Windsor and Maidenhead

BRITAIN'S RAILWAY DISASTERS

Fatal Accidents from the 1830s to the Present Day

Michael Foley

www.michael-foley-history-writer.co.uk

WHARNCLIFFE
TRANSPORT

First published in Great Britain in 2013
by Wharncliffe Transport
an imprint of
Pen and Sword Books Ltd
47 Church Street
Barnsley
South Yorkshire S70 2AS

Copyright © Michael Foley, 2013

ISBN 978 1 78159 379 0

The right of Michael Foley to be identified as the author
of this work has been asserted by him in accordance
with the Copyright, Designs and Patents Act 1988.

A CIP record for this book is available from the British Library

Printed and bound in England
by CPI Group (UK) Ltd, Croydon, CR0 4YY

Typeset in Minion by
CHIC GRAPHICS

Pen & Sword Books Ltd incorporates the imprints of
Pen & Sword Archaeology, Atlas, Aviation, Battleground, Discovery,
Family History, History, Maritime, Military, Naval, Politics, Railways,
Select, Social History, Transport, True Crime, and Claymore Press,
Frontline Books, Leo Cooper, Praetorian Press, Remember When,
Seaforth Publishing and Wharncliffe

For a complete list of Pen and Sword titles please contact
Pen and Sword Books Limited
47 Church Street, Barnsley, South Yorkshire, S70 2AS, England
E-mail: enquiries@pen-and-sword.co.uk
Website: www.pen-and-sword.co.uk

CONTENTS

ACKNOWLEDGEMENTS

To Linne Matthews for her hard work in editing this book. To www.railwayarchives.co.uk for helping me find the information on a number of the accidents, and to www.transporttreasury. co.uk for the use of some of their images.

NOTE ON ILLUSTRATIONS

Unless otherwise acknowledged, the pictures in this book are from the author's own collection of postcards, magazines and old photograph albums and it has been impossible to determine if any copyright is attached to them. Any infringement of copyright as a result of their publication is entirely unintentional; if any copyright has been infringed, the author extends his apologies to the parties concerned.

INTRODUCTION

Travelling by train would seem to be one of the safest ways to make a journey as trains run on rails, which in normal circumstances they do not leave. Early trains were quite slow in comparison with those of today so you'd think they would have been even safer. It will perhaps then come as a surprise to learn that there were numerous railway accidents resulting in fatalities from the early 1830s. In 1855 there was even a fatal accident involving the Royal Train.

There have been hundreds of fatal accidents since the arrival of rail travel in Britain. In the past there were scarcely any periods longer than a few months – in some cases weeks – when fatal accidents did not occur, although happily this is no longer the case.

Actual rail accident fatalities over the years number in the thousands. The accidents with the highest number of fatalities mainly took place in the twentieth century, including one incident in which more than 200 deaths occurred. Perhaps this was due to the increasing speeds that trains travelled at although high speed was not necessarily the cause of the accidents.

Although a very modern form of transport at its inception, in its early days the railways were ruled by ancient laws. One of these was the deodand – a fine that was charged on whatever caused a death, most usually a horse and cart at this time. In some early fatalities on the railways, the deodand was set at the value of the engine and train.

There was even a medical disorder related to train crashes from the nineteenth century known as 'railway spine', or Erichsen's Disease. Doctors began to notice similar symptoms occurring in those involved in railway accidents, including pain and sleeplessness. Sufferers often claimed damages through the courts; it seems that the compensation culture is not just a modern phenomenon.

Another feature of nineteenth-century railway accidents was the introduction of the term 'telescoping'. Its meaning is obvious in that a telescope slides into itself, one part into another. Unfortunately in relation to trains, it described how carriages slide into one another as the result of a collision, with obviously horrific effects on passengers.

There are some amazing stories connected with railway accidents. In one carriage of a train that crashed at Staplehurst in 1865 was a very famous passenger – Charles Dickens, who, ignoring his own safety went to the aid of several severely injured and dying passengers. Not many people realize how close the country came to losing one of its most famous authors and never knowing the works he penned after the crash.

Another strange connection with the same accident at Staplehurst was a lady who, after hearing of the crash, decided to travel back to London by Thames steamer rather than on the train. She was a passenger on the ill-fated *Princess Alice*, which collided with another ship and sank with hundreds of fatalities.

A good source of information on many of the early railway fatalities is contemporary newspapers. This is where much of the information in this book will come from. Unfortunately, the headlines in the Victorian press made those of today's tabloids look tame by comparison; if they were not always entirely factual, they were at least entertaining.

There was a strange similarity in many newspaper reports of accidents. It was clear that many different papers printed the same story. There was obviously some central source and in the 1890s reports began to be credited to telegram services such as Central News Telegrams and Press Association Telegrams.

Later accidents normally involved an official investigation and it is fascinating to see how the reports on these compare with newspaper stories about the accidents. There may well have been a limited number of causes of early railway accidents and it will be interesting to discover if any of those causes were repeated in later catastrophes.

CHAPTER 1

RAILWAY HISTORY

I think most people would, if asked, think of the nineteenth century as being the time of the beginning of the railways but the actual idea of running trucks on rails comes from a much earlier period. Rails were used to carry trucks in mines in Europe in the sixteenth century. The first British use of rails in mines came in the seventeenth century, with the trucks being pulled by horses or the miners themselves. The rails were made from wood rather than metal.

As most mines in Britain were in the north of the country this was where the majority of these early railways were situated. Railways were also used in other industries and a number of these were in the south. In the eighteenth century a small-scale stone quarry in Bath was transformed into a major commercial venture with the addition of a wooden railway to carry the stone. There was also an early railway at the chalk works at Purfleet in Essex in the eighteenth century.

The introduction of steam power for railways had its origins in the late eighteenth century. In 1784 Scottish inventor William Murdoch had built a steam road locomotive. The first working steam railway locomotive followed in 1804. It was built by Richard Trevithick and pulled a train from the Pen-y-Darren ironworks to Abercynon in Wales. Trevithick worked in the north of England after this, closer to most of the mines, and built other steam locomotives.

By the beginning of the nineteenth century there were numerous wooden railways in Britain. None of these carried passengers. In 1801 an Act was passed in Parliament for a line to be built from London to Portsmouth by the Surrey Railway Company. However, only a short section was built – from Wandsworth to Croydon. The trucks were horse-drawn and carried goods rather than passengers.

It is claimed that the Middleton Railway is the world's oldest continuously working railway. Coal had been dug at Middleton since the thirteenth century but was normally moved by water. In 1757 a wagonway was built towards Leeds. The following year an Act of Parliament ratified the railway. It was horse-drawn but the wooden lines were replaced with metal in the early nineteenth century.

In 1812 the Middleton became one of the first commercial railways to use steam locomotives. The first engine was the *Salamanca*, designed by Fenton, Murray and Wood, and it was the first commercial steam locomotive to operate successfully. Despite this the line was later returned to horse power after accidents occurred.

By the early nineteenth century there were a number of other small railways but the one that is often thought of as the first railway, the Stockton to Darlington, was actually the first passenger line to use steam engines. Although it was originally planned as a horse-drawn railway, George Stephenson persuaded the owners to use steam engines and it opened for business in 1825.

A very old engine from the Stockton to Darlington Railway – one of the very earliest engines used on the railway.

The railway had been originally built to connect a number of coal mines with Stockton and was at the time the world's longest railway. It was also the world's first publicly subscribed passenger railway and used horse-drawn vehicles as well as steam.

When the Manchester to Liverpool line was built in the mid 1820s the company directors were unsure about how to power it. One idea was for a stationary steam engine to pull the trucks by cable. After deciding to opt for mobile engines to pull the trucks, the company ran a competition to find a suitable steam engine.

In October 1829 *The Times* ran a story on the competition, which took place that month. In April 1828 the directors of the Liverpool and Manchester Railway had offered a prize of £500 for the best locomotive engine. The venue was Kendrick's Cross, which was 9 miles from Liverpool and one of the flattest parts of the line. A booth was erected for spectators and a band played to keep them amused. The crowd was estimated at around 15,000. The directors of the company arrived in a train pulled by Mr Stephenson's engine, which may have given him an advantage in the competition over other inventors.

The locomotives displayed on the first day were the *Novelty*, by Braithwaite and Ericson of London, the *Sans Pareil*, by Mr Ackworth of Darlington, and the *Rocket*, by Mr Robert Stephenson of Newcastle upon Tyne. Perhaps the most unusual engine entered for the competition was the *Cycloped*, by Mr Brandreth of Liverpool, which was worked by two horses. This was on a treadmill basis and only reached a speed of 4 miles per hour. More engines had been entered into the competition but did not turn up.

The report in *The Times* went on to state that the *Rocket* impressed everyone by travelling at 24 miles an hour with no carriages and then at 17 miles per hour pulling a load weighing – including its own weight – 17 tons. The *Novelty* was apparently even faster, travelling at 30 miles an hour and making everyone frightened for the safety of those on board. Humans were not used to travelling at such speeds! There were several other tests that the engines had to perform and it was the *Rocket* that was to be the winner.

Coal was still to play an even bigger part in the growth of railways. The use of tracks had been developed at coal mines but the need for coal in centres of the Industrial Revolution meant that better forms of carrying it to places like London were needed. Travel by sea, which was how most coal reached London, was slow, as was getting the coal from the mines to the sea.

The success of the Manchester to Liverpool line, especially its passenger business, was the spur to encourage further expansion of this new form of

ENGINE USED IN CONSTRUCTING THE LIVERPOOL & MANCHESTER RAILWAY, 1828-9.

One of the original engines used in the construction of the Liverpool and Manchester Railway. There was no protection for the driver on these early engines.

travel. By the mid-nineteenth century a number of passenger railways had come into existence around the country.

The cost of creating these new lines depended on the area they covered. Building some of the more difficult lines often led to the collapse of the company building them.

The introduction of viaducts and tunnels was another development of the new lines. Those that ran across the flattest routes were the least expensive to build but wherever the new lines appeared, along with them came crowds of railway navvies who would often invade quiet small villages until the line there was built and then they would move on along the tracks.

It has always been believed that the majority of these navvies were Irish but recent research has shown that many were English. Several of them were the same men who had built the canals. They would set up their own small towns with makeshift shacks. Many would spend their wages on alcohol and eventually they had to be given food tokens to ensure they would eat. They would often find themselves in debt to the companies that employed them.

The expansion of the railways in the nineteenth century was incredible, with around 1,500 miles of line laid in 1840, expanding to 6,000 miles by 1850 and 14,000 by 1875. The 1840s became known as the time of 'railway mania', a time of prosperity in the country. The Industrial Revolution was booming and many people had money to invest, including a growing middle class. Investment in railways seemed a safe option. Money was poured into railway companies and nearly 300 Acts of Parliament were passed to set up new companies in 1846. Many of these lines were never built because the companies went bankrupt or were bought out by larger organizations. Some companies that did build lines found they were unable to make a profit and by 1846 railway mania was over.

The largest railway companies began to take over the smaller ones and the railways became concentrated in the hands of a few companies. What railway mania had achieved, apart from causing many investors to lose their money, was to greatly expand the country's railway system. The biggest difference this made to the population was the speed with which travel could be undertaken. Destinations that had taken days to reach by stagecoach could now be reached within hours. An unforeseen benefit of the development of the railway network was that the sense of time became uniformly regulated across the country. Before this, different areas had worked to different times.

The new system was not without its drawbacks, however. The problem was, of course, that a number of different companies were running lines in different areas. Some concentrated their business into small, localized areas; others had lines that covered large parts of the country. Often different lines covered the same routes.

It was not the whole population who benefited from the expansion of the railways. The poor could rarely afford to travel on trains. It was only with the later introduction of cheap excursions that many more people could experience rail travel. The better off who did travel by train in the early days were often not happy with the price of fares, a commercial traveller's association even complaining about them.

By the mid-nineteenth century railway companies in Britain numbered in the hundreds, the smaller ones being taken over by larger companies throughout the century. Although the country was still covered by an enormous number of lines there was still no unified means of travelling from one area to another due to the lines being operated by so many separate companies. Even the gauge of the lines of each company was different. A standard gauge was agreed by Parliament in the middle of the century, but the Great Western Railway retained its wider gauge on some routes until 1892.

A unifying point for the railways came during the First World War when the Railway Executive Committee took control. This was made up of the managers of the main railway companies, who organized the system to carry the materials and men needed for the war effort. This also led to the restriction on different companies running on the same routes as the system became more streamlined.

The end of the war saw a return to the different rail companies competing with each other – often on the same routes, which led to a decrease in profits. The decline in coal exports also resulted in falling profits. The Railways Act of 1921 went some way towards dealing with these problems, when more than 100 companies were formed into four large groups: the London and North Eastern (LNER), London Midland and Scottish (LMS), Southern Railways (SR), and the Great Western (GWR). This was how things stayed until after the Second World War.

Once again, the government took over the railways when war began in 1939. Although the companies were guaranteed a level of payment, the damage due to bombing and lack of investment during the war years led to serious problems. The post-war Labour government was the final nail in the coffin for the private railways; the system was nationalized and British Rail was born.

According to this card this engine dates from 1840, which shows the rapid progress from the earlier engines. There is still little protection for the crew.

Although the railways did begin to make a profit after the war, by the late 1950s and early 1960s many local lines were poorly used and were eventually shut down by the famous Beeching Cuts. A number of rural areas lost their railway routes that had originated in the nineteenth century.

There was an about-turn in the 1990s, when the railways were privatized. The tracks became the responsibility of Railtrack. The freight service was sold off and the passenger service was divided between twenty-five franchises. But privatization has not been without its problems. After a number of difficulties, Railtrack was taken over by Network Rail in 2002. And the granting of contracts to the companies running the railways has not been without controversy – the events in 2012 involving Virgin Trains being one of the more ridiculous, when Virgin lost the West Coast franchise and were then re-awarded it due to shortcomings in the Department of Transport bidding process.

Despite these changes to the modern railway system, there do seem to be fewer serious accidents nowadays than there have been in the past, although when they do occur they can be very serious. Several studies have shown the numbers of those hurt or killed in rail accidents is only a very small proportion of the numbers that travel – which is little or no comfort to those who are involved in them.

CHAPTER 2

THE EFFECTS OF RAIL TRAVEL ON THE PERSON

In the early days of railways, there was a great deal of interest amongst those in the medical profession in the effects of rail travel on the person, especially in how the body reacted to accidents at high speed. People had never travelled at speeds such as those now possible in a train.

One of the early writers on the subject was John Eric Erichsen, later, Sir John. Erichsen was an eminent medical man who in subsequent years became a surgeon for Queen Victoria. He often appeared as a witness in court for the victims of railway accidents. He is best remembered today for saying that surgery on the abdomen, chest and brain was impossible.

One of the best-known books on the subject of injuries in rail accidents was Erichsen's *On Railway and Other Injuries of the Nervous System*, which comprised a collection of his lectures on spinal injuries. He was a well-known member of the Royal College of Surgeons when the book was published in 1867.

There was debate within the medical profession as to whether the common injuries seen amongst accident victims were due to physical injury to the spine or brain, or due to hysteria. Erichsen said that there were certain injuries of the spine that were caused by accidents of a trivial character. These were not entirely due to railway accidents but he claimed they had become more common since the introduction of railway transport and were often more severe amongst the victims of rail crashes.

Erichsen's lectures were aimed at doctors and he explained to them that members of the medical profession were to be increasingly called into the witness box in court cases where accident victims were claiming damages. He

The building of railways was big news in the nineteenth century. The building of this line in Betchworth, in Surrey, attracted a large crowd.

told his students that there were many cases in all walks of life and in science where there was uncertainty. Doctors should therefore go into court with confidence in their diagnoses despite opposition from other doctors employed by the railway companies. It was the job of the court to decide the truth. When they found in favour of the injured they often awarded very high damages for the time.

Erichsen went on to explain how these injuries had become known as 'railway spine' despite having similar symptoms to injuries from other causes. He had found that those injured often thought they were fine until sometime later. He then went on to detail individual cases, describing but not naming the victims.

The first involved a 43-year-old man who in a railway collision on 23 August 1864 was thrown forward and then back again. The man thought he was unhurt and even helped others escape from the wreckage. Later that evening he began to feel a tingling in his arms and legs. He became weak and depressed, had trouble walking, suffered headaches and his memory became impaired. There was also impairment of vision in one eye and hearing in one ear. When Erichsen saw him three months after the accident he was also suffering from some paralysis and could not bend down. The man was eventually awarded £6,000 damages at Worcester Assizes.

The next case was of a 43-year-old surgeon who was involved in a rail accident on 9 October 1864. The man was thrown forward in the collision but suffered no blows to his body. For three to four weeks there was no problem but then he began to have trouble concentrating, and walking tired him. By the time Erichsen saw him he had terrible pain, could not bend and suffered from hearing loud noises and seeing bright lights. A settlement of £2,500 was decided out of court.

The next example was also of a person shaken about during a rail accident without suffering a strike to any part of his body. The victim was a 50-year-old man described as stout but fit when the accident occurred on 3 February 1865. Although he was well just after the accident he soon became shaken and confused and had to see a doctor. It was fourteen months later that Erichsen saw him, by which time he had lost weight, was unable to walk far and had poor memory. He could not read for long, had bad dreams and could not bear loud noises. He also had poor vision in one eye. The case was heard at Gloucester Assizes in April 1866. It was the only case Erichsen mentioned where the railway company put forward powerful adverse medical testimony but the man still won £3,500 damages.

Although the symptoms in the first few examples were similar the next was very different. A man of thirty-three was thrown against the opposite side of the carriage during an accident on 1 March 1865. He then suffered from a stammer, a stiff spine and sensitive skin on his back, and could only walk sideways as he was unable to put one foot in front of the other. Damages of £4,750 were awarded at the Guildhall in December 1865. His condition later improved after salt baths.

Another of Erichsen's examples was of a victim of the Staplehurst accident on 9 June 1865. This was the one in which Charles Dickens was a passenger. It was also the only example of a female victim. A lady of twenty-eight was trapped in a stream under a dead woman and wreckage of the train for two and a half hours, with her neck at an unnatural angle. When rescued she could not support her head, which would fall onto her breast. When lying down she could not raise her head at all without using her hands to support it. She did recover somewhat but had to wear a stiff collar as her head still tended to flop to the side. Damages of £1,350 were awarded at the Guildhall – a lower amount than the other cases perhaps due to the sex of the victim.

The last example was of a 35-year-old man who suffered a cut lip during

THE GREAT RAILWAY GUY FOR 1849.

Not everyone saw the introduction of railways as a serious matter. This cartoon shows the so-called
Railway King, Mr Hudson, who was instrumental in opening the York to London line.

a rail accident on 4 November 1884. The man was shaken but was well enough
to continue his journey. Then a friend of his said that the man could not
remember the way home as he approached the area where he lived. He went
to bed when he got home and had to call a doctor a few days later.

Erichsen saw him fourteen months later and he looked much older than
he was, had a bad memory, could no longer add up and had bad dreams. The
man could also not read for long, was nearly blind in one eye and deaf on one

side. He could only walk with the aid of a stick. Damages of £6,000 were awarded at Worcester Assizes.

Erichsen went on to give a general sketch of the symptoms of concussion of the spine caused by rail accidents. There was, he said, a variety in the period in which the symptoms appeared; some occurred instantly while others only became apparent weeks later. There were mental and physical changes noticed by friends and family of the victim, who was often described as not being the man he used to be. Many victims also continued to think that they had no serious injuries for some time after the accident. Symptoms included a pallid countenance with an anxious expression, defective memory, confused thoughts, no business aptitude, a change in temper for the worse, disturbed sleep patterns, headaches, poor vision and hearing and an impaired sense of touch.

Railway companies were obviously not happy with the claims in Erichsen's book although from his writing it seems that they did not always contest such cases.

In the same year that Erichsen's book was published another book on the subject also appeared. This was *Railways in their Medical Aspects*, by James Ogden Fletcher. This book argued against the findings detailed in Erichsen's book. Fletcher was the consulting surgeon to the Manchester, Sheffield and Lincolnshire Railway so one could be forgiven for thinking that the timing of the book's publication was not coincidental.

By the 1860s it appeared that the majority of cases against railway companies that went to court led to damages being paid. In many cases the rail companies tried to settle out of court and only fight those where they believed that the claimant was not above board. They would also use private investigators to research the claimant's claims.

There was some argument amongst the medical profession relating to railway injuries and in 1865 the *British Medical Journal* said that the profession had not gained much credit with the public by assisting rail companies in casting doubt on those injured in railway accidents.

At about the same time that Fletcher wrote his book, Sir Charles Hall, a doctor acting for a railway company, was often asked to examine claimants. Hall said that he thought it right to look into the person's moral code and their probable motives alongside their symptoms.

In his book Fletcher displayed some sympathy with the view that railway accidents had a serious effect on their victims. He said that when he was appointed to the company he asked for medical equipment to be placed at regular sites alongside the lines to deal with the immediate effects of injuries

The Railway King came to grief as the bubble of railway mania began to burst. Perhaps the cartoon shows that not everyone was sad about this.

that he expected to see. He then said that these were never used. Fletcher also raised some of the general questions about the railways that were being discussed, such as, were they a necessity or a luxury? Did they contribute to or arise from increased civilization? The more important question for him, however, was: was there any evidence of injurious effects on the public?

In answer to the first question Fletcher claimed that the speed of travel possible on railways made it a necessity rather than a luxury as it connected all parts of the country together. It had also added to civilization by creating new towns and villages around the centres of the railway industries.

As to the health question, Fletcher argued that there was no evidence of negative effects of rail travel on the person. He proved this by examining a number of commercial travellers who on average made 500 to 600 rail journeys per year, normally in Second or Third Class – thought to be the most dangerous parts of a train in which to travel.

There were 200 travellers involved in Fletcher's study, some of whom had been working for twenty years. He found no disease peculiar to these men caused by rail travel. He also argued that rail employees suffered few problems caused by rail travel, although drivers and firemen did suffer from the effects of cold wind in the open engines.

It seems as if Fletcher was approaching the problem from a different perspective here. Erichsen was concentrating on accident victims while Fletcher was looking at the effects of rail travel itself.

Fletcher claimed that rail accidents could be avoided with proper care and attention and had it not been for Lord Campbell's Fatal Accidents Act of 1846, which decreed that for the first time relatives of people killed as a result of other people's actions could be awarded damages, accidents would occur more frequently. Perhaps he meant that before the passing of the Act the rail companies did not take such care over prevention of accidents, although this is unlikely given his views on rail travel not being to blame for some specific health problems.

It was a common belief amongst the public that rail companies displayed a lack of care. This had led to juries reusing the ancient awards of deodands in the case of accidents, which could make the company pay damages equal to the value of a train involved in an accident that resulted in death. The original idea of the deodand was that the item that caused a death would be given to the crown or local lord of the manor, sold and the money applied to charitable causes. It was this that led to the Fatal Accidents Act 1846, also known as the Lord Campbell Act. This Act removed the use of deodands and replaced them with damages. This meant that victims would now receive the

The fall of the Railway King, Hudson, left an opening for his replacement by Lord George Bentinck. Politician and racehorse owner Bentinck had big ideas on railway development.

payments. Perhaps it was this Act that alerted the medical profession to a possible lucrative interest in rail accidents.

The Act did not allay public fears about safety on the railways and the number of accidents was obviously causing concern. A letter to *The Times* from someone calling himself 'A Shareholder' in December 1853 put the case for the public. He asked if the public were any better off with the modern system of traffic when each week the papers were full of 'dreadful accounts of accidents and collisions throughout the country'.

He went on to claim that in the past a traveller made his will and prepared to be attacked and robbed, or even killed, when travelling by road. His opinion was that the trains travelled too closely together on the same lines. They often seemed to follow each other at intervals of only two to three minutes, which seemed reckless. The writer suggested that the use of danger signals between each station might benefit safety.

Fletcher believed many of the injuries that occurred on railways were due to the irresponsible behaviour of passengers. He quoted the Board of Trade returns for 1 January 1850 to 31 December 1854, which gave the number of people killed on the railways as 195. He then claimed that 106 of these were killed due to their own misconduct or for want of proper caution. Railway safety was not in the hands of the railway company but in the hands of the passenger, he said, although I think he was referring to accidents on the railways other than crashes. He went on to say that more deaths were likely to be caused by passengers getting out of trains before they stopped due to the fact that carriage doors were no longer always being locked or if they were locked, some passengers had their own keys. Carriage doors had been locked from the early times of the railways (although very early carriages had no doors). There is no clear date to determine when this practice was stopped; there were cases of locked doors being reported into the twentieth century.

One of the central themes of the book was that there were very few deaths in comparison with the number of passengers using the rail network. There are tables in the book showing the number of deaths on the railways other than those that occurred as a result of accidents. Perhaps one of the more interesting facts to emerge is that, amongst the population of London between 1851 and 1860, there were twice as many people hung every year than died in railway accidents.

The real purpose of the book seems to have been to disprove the claims made by Erichsen. Fletcher claimed that a number of deaths occurring a number of months after the victim had been involved in a rail accident, and were supposedly caused by the effects of the accident, could actually be blamed on other reasons. Many of the symptoms that had supposedly led to death, he said, had in fact dated from before the accident rather than them being caused by it.

One example that Fletcher gave was of a man who had seven doctors find that his illness was due to a rail accident, whereas he was actually suffering from alcohol abuse. He went on to blame long-lasting problems for those who had broken bones in accidents on poor quality beds in their homes.

The most important attack on Erichsen was in relation to his belief that damage to the nervous system was caused by rail crashes. Fletcher claimed that it was a surgical fact that the nerve centres were protected from injury in a remarkable way. This only changed when railway cases frequently became the subject of litigation.

Fletcher's main argument was that Erichsen's views in his book were not supported by enough evidence. He had only given details of six cases. Fletcher set out a table of 175 cases he had examined. Unlike Erichsen, he found that the vast majority of those involved in railway accidents were fully recovered within a few months.

Of Fletcher's 175 cases all but six had recovered enough to return to work. Of the others, one stopped work due to bronchitis and another due to varicose veins. The other four, he did admit, were not able to work due to the accident but in two cases this was due to a leg being shorter after it was broken. Another was due to a weak leg and the last was due to blindness resulting from the accident. There was no mention of any accident victim suffering from damage to the spine or nervous system that made them unable to work.

By the year 1892, much more was known about railway injuries; a book on the subject, called *Railway Injuries*, was published by Herbert Page. He put forward the view that many of the problems suffered by railway accident victims were due to emotional rather than physical injuries.

The availability of compensation as a reason for an increase in injury claims has already been mentioned. This was not confined to Britain. Page stated that after a law that awarded compensation was passed in Germany, the number of complaints increased enormously. This could of course be because people did not bother to complain before the law was passed as there was no point.

Page did not believe that the majority of cases that went to court were examples of malingering. He described accidents where people who suffered physical injuries often recovered after a few months. There were others, however, who suffered what Page called General Nervous Shock, brought about by functional or dynamic disturbance of nervous equilibrium rather than structural damage of the body. This was caused by the suddenness of the injury, not its severity. In many cases there was only slight or even no injury suffered at the time of a railway accident but the problems developed later. Page compares two similar accidents, one a rail crash and one that had

Lord George Bentinck thought that a way to help with the famine in Ireland was to loan them £16 million to develop their railways.

occurred in the street. He argued that a higher level of shock was suffered in the rail crash. This was due to fear and alarm. He gave an example of a man who was distraught after a train ran over his foot. It was then discovered that the only damage had been to the heel of his boot.

Page claimed that shock was often worse in those less seriously injured.

This seemed to be especially the case in serious accidents where others were badly hurt, reinforcing Erichsen's observation that some crash victims could help others escape from a wreckage and only later find themselves to be very ill.

One of Page's cases was of a man of forty-six who was tall and powerfully built. He suffered slight bruising in a rail accident but a friend sitting next to him on the train was killed. The man was plunged into a state of depression and could not eat or sleep. Fifteen months after the accident he was still in a weak and feeble state, was prone to cry and could not work.

The symptoms of this type of injury were, according to Page, sleeplessness, headache, nervousness, sweating, fear of strong light, and poor memory and appetite – similar to many of those symptoms mentioned by Erichsen. In another of Page's cases, a man with no sign of physical injury became very nervous and died thirty-seven days after the accident in which he was involved.

Another fatality was a young girl who, although not hurt in a railway crash, woke the following night screaming that the engine was coming into her room. The girl died five weeks later.

Page attributed this type of illness to fright, which caused changes in the nervous system. It was not something that affected everyone but many of those who did suffer were predisposed to its symptoms and had suffered some form of mental or emotional disorder before the accident.

As suggested in all the books I have mentioned, the matter of compensation came into it. Page gave an example of a mother of seven who, despite having no sign of physical injury, spent months in bed at home or in hospital suffering from pain and paralysis. This went on for six months before she was awarded compensation. Two weeks later, she had recovered. Page argued that this woman was not malingering as it was possible for an experienced doctor to tell if someone was malingering. He gave an example of a man who couldn't move one arm after a rail crash who when denied compensation threw both arms in the air and said, 'I'm ruined.'

Although Page denied that some people were malingering or falsely claiming injury, he did make an interesting comment. He said that some sufferers did not make an effort to get well until after their court claim was heard.

In 1905 Doctor Allan Hamilton published a book intended for use by doctors and lawyers in court – *Railway and Other Accidents with Relation to Injury and Disease of the Nervous System, a Book for Court Use*. The book listed seventy-three case examples. Hamilton claimed that the book was suitable for those who had previously had to deal with treatises of one extreme view or another. He had thirty years' experience of dealing with accidents and agreed that shock could induce a notable alteration in mental health.

Throughout the nineteenth century there were many concerns about the safety of rail travel, not only amongst the public but also amongst those in the medical profession, who seemed to side with one view or another depending on who was employing them. The introduction of the Fatal Accidents Act of 1846 obviously had a great impact on the treatment of and research into the effects of railway accidents. It opened a great deal of debate between those with differing views. It may also have had some effect on how hard the railway companies tried to avoid accidents.

CHAPTER 3

EARLY FATALITIES

It has been claimed that the first member of the public to be killed by a locomotive was a 13-year-old boy named John Bruce. He was killed in February 1813 when running along the tracks of the Middleton Railway. *The Leeds Mercury* reported that the accident would be a warning to others. There were undoubtedly other railway fatalities before this. There were supposedly two fatalities of young boys as early as 1650 on a coal railway in Whickham, County Durham. However, John Bruce does seem to have been the first person killed by a steam train.

The Middleton Railway was also the site of a further fatal accident in 1818. The boiler of a *Salamanca* steam locomotive exploded, killing the driver. According to the press, he was thrown 100 yards into an adjoining field. When a further fatality occurred in 1834 due to an explosion the line reverted to horse power.

The danger of steam engines was not confined to the railways or to the early engines. In 1847 the Thames steamer *Cricket* exploded near Hungerford Bridge. Of the seventy people on board, twenty were injured, one of whom died from injuries sustained in the explosion; three others drowned. An example of how the press liked to build the story up to greater heights at that time, the following day's *The Daily News* stated that 'the surface of the river was literally covered with bodies.' *The Daily News* had been founded in 1846 by Charles Dickens, who briefly served as the paper's editor.

Fatalities were often due to human error and the worst publicity possible occurred on the opening of the Manchester to Liverpool Railway in September 1830 when Mr Huskisson, MP for Liverpool, died in an accident. The opening ceremony was overseen by the Duke of Wellington so it was already bound to be a very public event.

The railway consisted of two tracks. During the opening ceremony one was used for an engine and three carriages carrying the Duke and the VIPs accompanying him. The other track had engines pulling four or five carriages with members of the public who were attending the event.

According to *The Times* a few days after the event, the members of the Duke's party were warned not to leave the carriages during stops for fuel or water. However, when the *Northumbrian* engine pulling the VIP train stopped for water a number of gentlemen got out to inspect the track and the train. There was a 4- to 6-foot gap between the lines and two engines, the *Phoenix* and the *North Star*, passed safely on the other line while the men were outside the train.

Then the *Rocket* was seen approaching them at some speed, 25 to 30 miles per hour, which led to a panic. Most of the men managed to either climb back into the carriage or move to the other side of the train. It seems that the steps that would normally have been at the side of the carriages by the doors had been removed from the royal carriage and temporary ones placed at the rear. Mr Huskisson, who had been talking to the Duke, who was still on the train, fell and was injured by the train running over his leg. The injury to his leg was so severe that it was decided it had to be amputated. The report went on to state that Mr Huskisson spoke to say that he was a dead man and that he should be left alone to die, but he was persuaded that he should be moved into the orchestral carriage, where a band had been playing to amuse the guests.

The victim was then taken to the home of his friend, the Reverend Blackburn, in Eccles. The Reverend had in fact been on the train but was unaware of what had happened until they arrived at his home. It was decided that although amputation was needed, the victim could not cope with the operation. He died shortly afterwards.

There was a slightly different version of events in *The Examiner* the day after the report in *The Times*. According to this report Mr Huskisson went to grab the door to the carriage, which was then struck by the *Rocket*, which knocked him to the ground. *The Examiner* report also seemed to slightly underestimate the effect of the accident saying that it 'threw a damp over the subsequent proceedings.'

November 1832 was to see a fatal accident at Rainhill Station. A Second Class train left Manchester at 7.15 am and was to stop at Rainhill at nine o'clock to pick up more passengers travelling to Liverpool. While waiting to pick up passengers the eight o'clock train from Manchester appeared, travelling at great speed, which it must have done to have caught up to the previous train.

There was no way of stopping the oncoming train but by moving the stationary train the force of the collision was lessened. The engine of the eight o'clock train hit the rear of the previous train and knocked some of the carriages off the track. The engine then hit the station building, destroying the front of the station. One man was killed instantly. Several of the carriages of the first train were badly damaged but there were no other fatalities.

A different type of accident happened in December 1836 on the Newcastle and Carlisle Railway. There were three fatalities, along with a great deal of damage to property. It took place near the Corby Bridge across the river Eden. Just beyond this is a viaduct crossing the valley of the Corby Beck. On the western end there was a short branch line leading to a coal staithe with points off the main line.

On 3 December a train from Newcastle to Carlisle with twenty-six passengers was travelling through the area. As he approached the branch line the driver of the *Samson* locomotive saw that the points were set towards the staithe instead of the main line. He reversed the motion of the engine and he and the fireman jumped off. The train hit six empty coal trucks and forced them off the line. The engine and some of the goods carriages fell down about 8 feet as the staithe collapsed. The passenger carriages stopped before the drop and despite one carriage being damaged, none of

A postcard showing the copy of a memorial at Ely Cathedral to two men who died in a railway accident in 1845. The words seem to point out that the railways were godly to some.

the passengers seemed badly hurt. However, one man who had been standing on the staithe fell as it collapsed and he died the next day. Later, two boys of fourteen and sixteen were found dead between the fallen goods trucks. It was not known that they were there or even how they got on the train.

Newspaper reports on the accident continued for some time. The reports on 14 December in both *The Morning Chronicle* and *The Morning Post* were very similar. They were also very descriptive, describing a nearby bridge as 'a noble bridge'. They also both mentioned how the driver, to 'his horror and consternation saw that the points were set for the staithe.'

There must have been some level of copying of reports in different newspapers as *The Blackburn Standard* a week later, on 21 December, also stated that the driver saw 'to his horror and consternation that the points were set to the staithe.'

CHAPTER 4

1840 to 1850

The Great Western Railway was formed in 1833 and ran its first trains in 1838. Its engineer was Isambard Kingdom Brunel, who introduced the broad gauge railway that the company used for many years. After GWR took over some other companies in the mid-eighteenth century they operated both broad and narrow gauge lines.

It was to be 1892 before they finally abandoned the broad gauge altogether. Known by some as God's Wonderful Railway, it was also responsible for a number of early accidents that sent some of its passengers to meet its namesake. Although these accidents were reported in the newspapers there did not seem to be the same sensational headlines focussing on the number of accidents on the GWR as there were on other rail companies.

The first accident I found reporting on the GWR was in June 1840, concerning a fire on a goods train. The article, in *The Times,* stated that reports circulating in London were 'varied and extraordinary'. It went on to say that *The Times*'s reporter was in high regard of the company and received authentic particulars. Perhaps the fact that the reporter was in high regard of the company was the reason for a lack of sensationalist headlines about its accidents.

The accident involved a goods train that left Paddington at 11.00 pm with twenty-nine tarpaulin-covered trucks. As it reached Acton Cutting, a watchman on the line noticed that one of the trucks was on fire. His warning was not heard by the driver. By the time the driver had noticed, the fire had spread to another truck. They then detached the two burning trucks and removed some of the goods with help from locals attracted by the fire. Another engine arrived to take the train on its route. The original engine then removed the burning trucks to Ealing as there was no water available at Acton Cutting. Unfortunately, there was also no water at Ealing so the trucks were left to burn.

The Times's reporter commented that the lower class of labourers who gathered to watch the fire did nothing to help and actually cheered as the trucks were destroyed. It would seem that there was little sympathy for goods carried by rail. It was noticed that one of the labourers had a bulky appearance and was found to have 75 yards of cloth wrapped round his body, illustrating that rail accidents often presented an opportunity for theft.

The fire was apparently not an unusual event on the railways. The report ended by saying that the previous week the train on the London to Birmingham route had caught fire. That fire had been on a passenger carriage carrying luggage on the roof, which had caught fire. Although all eighteen passengers escaped it is apparent that fire fighting was not a priority on the early railways.

The fatal accident on the Hull and Selby Railway on 7 August 1840 was reported in *The Times*. The accident took place near Howden Station. A police constable saw that a large metal item on the carriage behind the engine had moved and was hanging over the edge of the carriage. He tried to warn the driver but it was too late. The item fell onto the track causing the following carriages to come off the tracks and turn over.

The report went on to describe the passenger carriages behind the one carrying the metal object. It showed how the danger from accident was greater to those travelling with cheaper tickets. The first carriage behind the goods one was a Third Class carriage with no cover. There was nothing to stop the passengers being thrown out if the carriage overturned, which it had done.

Behind the Third Class carriage was a Second Class one. It had a cover, which gave some protection, but no sides. Behind this was a First Class carriage, which had a cover as well as sides. In all there were five deaths.

The report of the inquest for the accident in *The Times* went into the injury details of three of the bodies. The condition of the bodies was so terrible that they could not be recognized. One of them was identified by his cousin but he admitted that it was difficult to recognize him. The identifications were confirmed by what the three victims had in their pockets.

The piece of metal that had fallen off the carriage and caused the accident was said to have weighed about 3 tons. The rope that had tied it to the carriage had worn through as a result of movement when the train was moving. The engine and the first truck, which had held the metal, were still on the track but the next seven carriages were off the track and smashed to pieces.

The train driver said that after passing Howden Station the engine suddenly speeded up. Looking round he saw that the carriages had been left behind after the metal had come loose, causing the following carriages to be thrown off the track.

William Greaver, the guard on the train, said that the passenger carriages on the train had been at the rear, with the goods carriages between them and the engine. He said that this was seen to be the safest position for passengers in case anything went wrong with the engine. If the engine was derailed then the carriages at the back would be the safest. This would seem to make sense. Unfortunately, in this case it didn't because the metal that fell from the first carriage caused the ones following, including the passenger carriages, to become derailed.

The Morning Post of 10 August explained that it was their 'melancholy and painful duty to report on the accident'. According to their report so many accounts of the accident had been contradictory that they had sent their own reporter to find the facts so that their readers would have every particular presented to them.

There was a very rapid settlement for the accident when on 14 August the jury at the enquiry awarded a deodand of £500 – the value of the whole train, including the engine. The awarding of deodands was to become common practice over the next few years. This was far from popular with the rail companies.

A report on the accident was written for the Board of Trade by Lieutenant Colonel Frederick Smith, the Inspector General of the Railways. The report went into details about the carriage that had been thrown off the tracks first. It was a Leeds and Selby Railway First Class carriage. This had been positioned behind the engine, tender and a truck carrying the item that fell onto the tracks.

This differs to what was written in newspaper reports that said that a Third Class carriage was first behind the truck. The carriage was broken to pieces but had fortunately been empty. The deaths occurred among the passengers in the sixth carriage – a Hull and Selby Second Class carriage – although the carriage itself was not badly damaged.

There was a fatal accident on the Eastern Counties railway on 17 August 1840. *The Times* published a witness statement relating to the accident a few days later. The passenger, Mr Cerebauld, was in a Second Class carriage when it began to sway from side to side. He mentioned that he had never seen a train go so fast. He then found himself in a cornfield and believes that he was thrown out of the carriage.

An inquest was held sometime after the accident and although only one man had died at the time of the catastrophe two more had died since, including the engine driver. The jury was told that the accident was caused by the speed that the train was travelling as it went towards Brentwood in Essex.

There is quite a steep gradient on the line leading to Brentwood and other drivers who worked on the line reported that they would normally shut off the steam at that part of the journey. As the previous witness statement had said that the train was travelling very fast – perhaps as fast as 60 miles an hour – the coroner instructed the jury to decide if this was the cause of the accident, despite not being able to hear evidence from the driver because he was dead.

The Examiner of the 23 August wrote a report of the accident that appeared to be a copy of many previous reports in other newspapers. Even the headline, 'Dreadful Railway Accident', was the same that a number of newspapers had used, not only for this accident but for many others.

If the driver had lived and it was found that he was to blame he would have been charged with manslaughter. The jury returned a verdict of accidental death. They then awarded a deodand of £500 on the value of the engine.

A more serious accident took place on the GWR on 25 October the same year. The *Fire King* engine ran into the carriage house and a coke truck at Farringdon Road Station. The driver had apparently forgotten to let off the steam and put the drags on as the train came into the station.

The driver and the guard were killed instantly; the driver's head reportedly was 'smashed to atoms'. There were only four passengers, two of whom suffered broken limbs. The other two were severely bruised. The stoker escaped unhurt but was unable to say why that was.

There was also another account on the same page that named the deceased as James Ross, driver, and Marlow, guard. The guard supposedly shouted a warning as the train approached the station without slowing down. The report went on to say that Ross, a single man, had been working for the company for two years and was a reliable worker. Marlow was a widower with two young children aged eight and ten. It was expected that the railway company would make some provision for the support of the children.

At the inquest, held at the Railway Tavern at Farringdon Road Station, the stoker on the train, James George James, said that he was sure the driver had been sober on the night of the accident. He had known and worked with him for five months. The driver had been standing at his normal position when the stoker noticed they were by the station. He called to the driver and applied the brake on the tender. He received no answer from the driver and was then thrown off the engine by the force of the collision. According to his evidence the cause of the accident was the driver's failure to turn off the steam.

Further evidence from the constables and others employed on the station stated that they shouted at the driver as he failed to slow down. They said that it seemed as though he was asleep on the engine.

Another witness to the accident was the company's chief engineer, Mr Brunel. He told the inquest that the train approached the station at about 15 miles per hour, which was normal for a goods train. He was surprised when it did not slow down.

Press reports on the accident did not always appear to be accurate, as related in a letter that appeared in *The Times* in September 1841. The letter writer had been a passenger on the mail train from Bath and he was disputing the report in the newspaper of an accident involving that train. He felt bound not to allow the public to be kept in the dark about the truth of the accident, saying that this was the wish of all the persons involved with the railway. He claimed that whenever an accident occurred, the railway did their upmost to keep it as secret as possible.

According to the writer it was normal practice for a policeman to be on duty during the day at certain distances along the route. Before the train reached him and until it passed the policeman would hold out his hand to show that all was alright. If this was necessary during the day, he declared, it must have been even more so at night and yet he had seen no policeman for the whole of his journey.

The writer also suggested that where there were embankments on the railway line there should have been someone responsible for checking that they were safe. These men should also have been on duty day and night. If this had been the case, he said, this accident would not have occurred. He also complained about the report in *The Times*, which stated that there were two engines on the train, one at the front and one at the rear. Both engines had actually been at the front, otherwise when the first engine had struck the obstruction, the other engine would have continued on and crushed all the carriages in between.

The accident had happened about 3 miles beyond Chippenham. When the train crashed, the carriages in front of the one in which the letter writer had been in folded one within another like a telescope. He said that the cries and moans for help were dreadful, although when he went on to list the injuries to the passengers there were few and none seemed to be very serious.

The previous day's report in *The Times* did not vary from the letter writer's report of events. The only difference I could find was that he said that the guards were injured, while *The Times* said that they were only shocked and had returned to work. Perhaps the writer did have a fair point about the railway companies trying to keep details of accidents quiet but on this occasion I can't see that he was justified in claiming that the report in *The Times* was different from his own.

Apart from injuries resulting from accidents involving collisions and derailments there were often injuries caused by people being hit by trains. Some were obviously members of the public but there have also been numerous incidents of railway workers being hit and killed by trains. In some cases these were possibly the result of a lack of training for the workers.

The London and Birmingham Railway began operating in 1833. It was to have a short lifespan because in 1846 it became part of the London and North Western Railway, although while it was in existence a fatal accident occurred.

On 12 November 1840 there was a collision between two trains at Harrow. The first reports said that there had been thirty to forty deaths. The actual number was much lower. In fact, there were only two fatalities. *The Times's* report of 13 November stated that they were unable to find out any further information due to profound secrecy and even insults from the company.

What quickly became evident, despite the reluctance of the company to give out any information, was that trains into Euston had stopped running. The station was said to have been almost deserted as all employees had been sent to the site of the accident.

It was to be 16 November before details of the accident were published in *The Times*. By this time an inquest had been set up at the Queen's Head tavern near Harrow Weald under Mr Wakely MP. Although there had been two deaths it was thought that the stoker of engine No. 82 was also unlikely to survive his injuries.

The Standard of 16 November reported on how the bodies of the two deceased were at the Queen's Head tavern in the same state as they had been discovered. What this state was could not be ascertained until the remains had been inspected by the jury.

The general view of the collision seems to be that whoever was responsible for giving warning to the train bound for Euston did not give it soon enough for the train to stop before it hit another train on the same line. It was also reported that another train had only just managed to stop before running into the wreckage on the line.

Although there had been high value deodands awarded in some previous accidents it was not always the case that a high deodand was awarded. After an accident on the Birmingham and Gloucester Railway the man in charge of the enquiry informed the jury that the company had taken every precaution and they should apply a nominal deodand. They followed his instructions and awarded a deodand of one shilling.

The Dee Bridge disaster. Five people died when the bridge failed and the train fell into the river. A collapsed bridge was not an uncommon event in the nineteenth century.

In between the two reports on the accidents that shut the line to Euston there was a report of another on the York and North Midland Railway. This railway had begun operations in 1839 and continued until 1854, when it amalgamated with a number of other small companies to form the North Eastern Railway.

The accident occurred when a passenger train from Leeds collided with a luggage train near the junction with the Leeds and Selby Railway at Milford. The first report stated that two people had died instantly while a number of others were badly mutilated. Two of the carriages on the passenger train were smashed to pieces.

Further reports explained that the passenger train was en route to Hull when it was hit by a coal train that had for some reason stayed longer than expected on the main line. The carriages destroyed were the First Class ones. According to the report one casualty had his face taken off by the broken carriage and died on the spot. An elderly lady had her hand cut off and died shortly afterwards. One lady in the Third Class carriage jumped out before the collision and was unhurt. The Third Class carriage was one of the least damaged so she need not have leaped. The accident caused consternation in the city of York, according to *The Morning Chronicle* of 14 November.

An incident that occurred in September 1841 at the Box Tunnel near Bath is another that could be attributed to a lack of training. A gang of men had been working for a week in the tunnel removing ballast. There were about thirty to forty men at work when two trains passed in the tunnel hitting two of the men, injuring one of them fatally.

The inquest was held at the Three Tuns Inn in Bath. The coroner was Mr English and a solicitor, Mr Napp, appeared for the GWR. The company was always represented by a solicitor whilst the victims rarely were.

One of the surviving labourers who had been working in the tunnel, Eli Sainsbury, gave his version of what occurred. He had been working in the tunnel for a year and a half. He said that the accident was caused by two trains meeting in the tunnel and the workers had not known what to do to get out of their way. Sainsbury was told that if the watchman told them to clear the road they would normally get onto the other side of which the train was travelling. The watchman would tell them to clear the north or the south road accordingly. Because there were two coming at the same time they were unsure of what to do. There were a few seconds between the trains passing so Sainsbury and another man stood in the centre of the tracks and jumped to the other when the first one had passed. The man who was killed was between the passing train and the wall and was hit by the train. The only instructions he had received when he went to work in the tunnel were to get out of the way when he heard the watchword.

Sainsbury went on to claim that there was not room to stand between a train and the wall of the tunnel as it passed. There were niches in the wall for the watchmen to get into as a train passed but there were none near where the men were working at the time of the accident. He had never known two trains to pass so closely together in the tunnel before.

Another man, John Wilkins, had been standing near the deceased. He had heard the signal to clear the north road given by the watchman. As he got off the north road he heard almost immediately the instruction to clear the south road. He said that he hardly knew what to do as they thought both trains would meet. Wilkins then pressed himself against the south wall, as did the man who had died and the other man who was injured. He said that there was a great deal of confusion amongst the men in the tunnel.

An assistant engineer for the company, James Sherriff, said he was well

A new bridge was built across the Dee after the disaster when a bridge collapsed while a train was going across the river. It looks much sturdier than the old bridge.

acquainted with the tunnel and there was room to stand against the wall when a train passed. There was also room to stand in the middle of the tracks as two trains passed each other. The centre space was 6 feet wide but the steps of the carriages were 2 feet wide, so this left a 2-foot gap in the centre. It would mean, however, that a person would have to know they were in the centre. Sherrif said that they told railway employees to lie down if two trains passed at the same time.

The coroner said he did not see that any blame could be attributed to the company. It was an accident arising from the confusion of the men because two trains had met in the tunnel.

There was an interesting letter in *The Times* on 9 October 1841 concerning deodands. It stated that Earl Spencer, who was the Lord of the Manor of Wimbledon, had received a £300 deodand from the Southampton Railway Company in relation to a fatal accident that happened on his land. The money was due to the death of a young girl and the earl gave the money to her family. The fact that this was news shows this must have not been the norm.

There was another accident on Christmas Eve 1841 on the GWR when a luggage train from Paddington hit a collapsed embankment at Sonning Hill Cutting near Reading. The engine and its following carriage were derailed, causing the death of eight of the thirty-eight passengers on board.

There was a surprisingly quick response to the accident when a letter on the disaster appeared in *The Standard* on Christmas Day. The letter was an attack on the railway company for putting a passenger carriage next to the engine, airing the familiar argument as to where carriages were safest.

There were some interesting comments in *The Times*'s report on the accident, one being that owing to the strict reserve of the company's servants they had considerable trouble in collecting information on the accident. The report also stated that the passengers were of the 'poorer class'. It seems that the driver and the guard, who was in the same carriage as the passengers, managed to jump clear before the collision.

One of the questions raised about the accident was that the embankment that collapsed had not been in a secure condition. The cutting was very deep at that point and the soil was of a soft and springy nature and therefore more liable to fall – especially after the recent heavy rainfall. Apparently, representatives of the company had recently had their attention drawn to this. The company employee responsible for the area said he had examined the embankment at five o'clock the previous evening and it had been secure at that time.

There were also some questions about the position of the passenger carriage, as mentioned in the letter in *The Standard*. It was an open carriage and was positioned behind the engine. It had been argued that placing passengers in such a position on a luggage train – between the engine at the front and the goods vans at the back – put them in danger. If a collision occurred then the weight of the goods carried behind them would be forced onto the passenger carriage.

The report also commented that the identities of the deceased could not be established due to the secrecy enjoined on the company's servants. The newspaper called on the company directors to show compassion for the victims' families by affording every means in their power to reassure the public.

At the inquest there was again no legal representation for the victims. The finding was that the fatalities were due to accidental death, although comment was passed on the unstable embankment and the positioning of the passenger carriage.

There was mention of the inquest in *The Morning Chronicle* of 28

December. According to the report the inquest was held in a miserable shed at the back of a beer house. When one considers the important people that attended such events this is surprising.

Over the next few days there were several comments about the accident in *The Times* from various sources. Many were critical of the GWR, especially in relation to the position of the passengers. This led to a response from their engineer, Brunel. He stated that positioning the carriage behind the engine on a goods train was the safest option. This was because goods trains were slower than passenger trains and therefore more likely to be hit from behind by faster trains. If the passengers were at the rear this would put them in more danger.

There was a further inquest in relation to the accident when another of the passengers died in hospital. It was held at the Royal Berkshire Hospital for Richard Woolley before Mr Blandy, the coroner, who made a very interesting observation in his summing up. He said that there was a very strong feeling in the minds of the public that accidents of this nature should be blamed on the rail companies. He told the jury they should take into account that this new system of rapid travelling could not be adopted without proportionate risk. If there were no grounds for negligence on the part of the company they should not think in this way.

This subject was again mentioned in *Jackson's Oxford Journal* on 1 January; it was claimed that when accidents occurred where people were crushed like nuts in nutcrackers, the railway companies inevitably found that nothing was wrong. The report went on to say that another eight to ten people were likely to be crushed next week, as had happened last week, and it was perhaps time for a slow train that arrived safely instead of a fast train that did not.

The jury decided that the accident may have been avoided if there had been a night watch on the embankment. They also said that, in future, passenger trucks should be placed further from the engine.

The Board of Trade Report on the accident was compiled by Lieutenant Colonel Frederick Smith. It listed the number and order of the carriages that made up the train. It also gave the number of wheels of each carriage. Smith found that there was no error in the construction of the embankment that slipped but the spoil on top of the edge of the cutting may have been a contributing factor, although it had been there for two years. There had also been a number of small slips in the area.

Smith mentioned that he had recommended in 1840 that all carriages had buffers. The carriages on the train did not have them. Another criticism was of the Third Class carriages, which was where the fatalities took place. The design was not as good as the public should expect. The sides and ends were only 2 feet high. Passengers could be in these open carriages for ten to twelve hours, even at night.

News of an accident on the GWR reached Parliament in June 1845 and caused some excitement, according to *The Times*. There was a rumour circulating that a fast train to Exeter had left the line between West Drayton and Slough. Carriages had supposedly overturned and fallen down a steep embankment, causing several deaths.

There was of course limited long-distance communication at the time but it still seems surprising that the rumour that had reached Parliament could have been so exaggerated. It turned out that the accident was not anywhere near as serious as had been reported.

The London to Exeter train had only recently begun to run on the route. It was noted that the time that the journey took was an incredible four and a half hours for a journey of 200 miles.

The train in question was only a small one, with two First Class and two Second Class carriages. It had left Paddington at its normal time. As it reached Dog Kennel Bridge just before Slough the engine broke loose from the carriages, which then came off the line. Three of the carriages – the two First Class and one Second Class – then fell down the embankment.

There were about 150 passengers in the three carriages and many of them were trapped. In true newspaper fashion it was stated that one lady was so alarmed that for some time her life was seen to be in jeopardy. It was even at a late hour doubtful if she would ever be restored to a rational being. Eventually about forty people were taken to hospital with mainly non-serious injuries.

It seems that the accident was due to the luggage truck becoming derailed while still attached to the engine. It then struck a bridge, breaking it free from the engine and causing the passenger carriages to come off the line.

There was an interesting report on an accident in October 1845, when the Great Western Railway prosecuted a man who had nearly caused a serious accident. There were some workmen employed on a job near Bath. This involved crossing the track with wagons. The driver of one of these wagons was told to wait until the train due had passed but ignored this and crossed the line. The train hit the horses pulling the wagon and cut off one of the horses' legs. The wagon was thrown onto two men, causing serious injuries.

The wagon driver, Henry Salter, was not hurt. The following day he was brought up before the Bath magistrate. A charge was preferred against him by the superintendent of the GWR police, Mr Burton, under a clause of the company's own Act of Parliament. The prisoner was described as a loutish-looking man who could neither read nor write. He was fined £5 but given a month in prison in lieu of payment.

The magistrate then observed that the man did not look fit to be in charge of such an important job and that perhaps the contractor should have been fined for employing a man who was not up to it. The case also seems to show that rail companies were inclined to take a harsher line if mistakes were made by people, such as contractors, who were not their own employees.

There was an accident on the Eastern Counties Railway in December 1845. It took place near Thetford on Christmas Eve. The suspicion of an accident came about when a train failed to arrive at Norwich in the afternoon. It had left Shoreditch at eight o'clock that morning.

A reporter from *The Times* was shocked that information on such an accident that occurred during the day was not sent to its destination, where family members of the some of the passengers were likely to be waiting – especially after the mail train from Shoreditch due to leave there at 11.30 am also did not arrive.

It was not until eleven o'clock that evening that news arrived confirming the accident when the Norwich train that had left for London at 4.00 pm returned with the passengers from the crashed train and news that the driver and fireman had died.

The train had come off the line and fallen down an embankment. The driver died instantly; the fireman was terribly mutilated and died shortly afterwards. Surprisingly, none of the passengers were seriously hurt. If the accident had occurred a quarter of a mile further on then the train would have fallen into a river, with no doubt greater loss of life.

There was another fatality in January 1846 on the South Eastern Railway, which had its origins as far back as 1836. One of the difficulties with the route from London to Dover was bridging the river Medway. It was on a bridge that the accident occurred.

A goods train had left Dover at 8.00 am and was passing over one of the bridges in the Medway Valley between Tonbridge and Penshurst stations. Part of the bridge then collapsed and the engine, tender and one of the wagons fell from the bridge. The engine driver survived the fall but died shortly afterwards. The fireman survived with only slight injuries.

The bridge – a wooden structure standing on bricks – had been weakened during recent flooding and had been strengthened on its north side so that trains could still run across it.

The engine had fallen into the river and the driver and the fireman were later found on the bank as the fireman had swum ashore, pulling the driver behind him. The men turned out to be brothers, William and George Doyle. At this point the driver was still alive, despite serious injuries; according to the report he was almost cut in two and died shortly afterwards. The driver had jumped off the engine when the bridge began to collapse but was caught between the engine and tender, and that was what caused his injuries.

The use of deodands was by this time seen as a burden on the railway companies and also unfair as the money awarded was not for the victims or their families. It had in reality become no more than a fine on what the public saw as indifferent rail companies. A nominal sum was awarded in this case of one shilling, but changes were on the way.

The Fatal Accidents Act of 1846 was to lead to the right of an injured party to claim damages against railway companies. It was to bring unforeseen results for the medical profession.

There was a further fatal crash in September 1846 on the GWR as the Bristol train from Paddington reached Farringdon Road Station. As the train approached the station the steam was turned off and the brakes were applied. Then the luggage van, which was behind the tender, broke loose and ran off the rails. The following Second Class carriage then ran into the luggage tender and was demolished. Two of the passengers died instantly. Again, the report in *The Times* stated that due to the strict silence observed by the servants of the GWR the identities of the deceased were unknown.

The report went on to explain that the luggage truck was a small four-wheeled carriage similar to a horsebox and that it was too light to precede heavy six-wheeled passenger carriages. This would seem to be borne out by the accident in June the previous year, which was caused by a similar luggage van coming off the rails and hitting a bridge. Once again, it appeared that the positioning of different types of carriages could be a danger to passengers.

The inquest took place a few days afterwards, which was after the newspaper comments about the position of luggage vans. However, the investigation seemed to concentrate more on the condition of the luggage van and whether it was due to there being a fault in it that caused the accident. Once again, there was no proof of this being the case so a verdict of accidental death was given.

There was another fatal accident on the GWR in January 1847, near Southall Station, when two men died. The accident was most unusual and shows how fate can play a hand in who dies and who doesn't in such incidents.

The express from Exeter to Paddington was passing Southall Station at its usual high speed. Just as it passed the station the band of iron or tyre that surrounded the right driving wheel broke free. The tyre was 1½ inches thick and 23 feet in circumference. It broke into pieces and parts of it flew off in different directions.

Unfortunately, just as this happened another train was approaching the station from the opposite direction. The train had slowed down to stop at the station. Part of the tyre – about 7 feet in length and weighing 240lbs – landed on the Second Class carriage of the approaching train.

The first compartment was empty but there were six passengers in the second and the metal hit two of them, killing them instantly. They were Henry Bishop and Henry Halt. With no feeling for the men's families the report on the accident in *The Times* described how Halt's head was completely laid open and his brains were scattered about the carriage. The newspaper also related that the expression on his face was one of surprise. There were a few other slight injuries amongst the other passengers in the compartment, including Halt's brother. The dead men were sitting opposite each other when the metal came through the carriage.

During the coroner's inquest it was established that a similar accident had occurred with the engine, the *Queen*, a few months earlier when it was travelling at about 60 miles an hour. That time no one had been injured. An engineer, Mr Cubitt, said he believed that the tyre broke at the weld. A number of independent engineers gave the opinion that it would be better to fix the tyre with screws rather than weld them.

The coroner said that there could be no blame attached to the company but went on to point out that if this had happened as the train passed a crowded platform it could have killed about sixty people. One of the jury then enquired if the speed of trains was limited by law, and if it wasn't this was a great omission because if the driver of a coach or other vehicle was driven furiously then the driver would be liable for a penalty. The coroner replied that there was no limit to the speed of trains and that the public were to blame as the directors of railway companies found that they could scarcely satisfy the public in this respect.

There was a serious accident on the Shrewsbury and Chester railway in May 1847. A train had just left Chester Station on 24 May and had begun to cross the bridge across the river Dee. Part of the bridge then collapsed, plunging the train into the river. The chain holding the engine to the train snapped and the engine managed to reach the other side safely.

Berrow's Worcester Journal stated on 27 May that as a result of the accident Chester had been thrown into an unprecedented state of excitement and consternation. Although part of the bridge had come free, allowing the train to fall, none of the bridge had collapsed onto the top of the train, which would have made the situation even worse.

There was a witness statement from one of the passengers in *The Times*'s report of 26 May. The man's name was Proud and he told how he was in a carriage that turned upside down in the river. He managed to climb out of a window and swam to the shore. A number of passengers were rescued shortly after the accident occurred and surprisingly there were only five deaths.

Mr J. Hostage, the coroner, made an interesting comment at the inquest. He said that he might ask the jury if they thought it necessary to have a civil engineer survey the bridge. He advised that it was a good idea and that the civil engineer should be someone unconnected with any railway. He didn't think they ought to trust a government surveyor as the bridge had been passed by General Pasley, Inspector General of Railways.

Mr Munt of the Chester and Holyhead Railway said that General Pasley had resigned and that the likely government surveyor would be Captain Coddington. The coroner suggested a Mr Yarrow, who was an able engineer and unconnected with any railway or, it seems, the government.

Although the engine survived and managed to get across the bridge it was not entirely unscathed. The *Derby Mercury* of 26 May reported that the engine driver's last memory of the accident was of seeing the fireman lose his head as some part of the bridge appeared to strike him.

The London and North Western Railway was formed in 1846 with the merger of the London and Birmingham Railway, the Manchester and Birmingham Railway and the Grand Junction Railway, which had already taken over the Liverpool and Manchester Railway. The company continued to take over other railways.

Accidents began to be reported soon after the formation of the company. There was one as early as November 1846 at Chelford Station, although there were no deaths. In the same month the company had to pay £300 damages to an injured passenger.

The accidents became more serious, with seven deaths in June 1847 at Wolverton Station. The mail train for Liverpool, with nineteen carriages, had left Euston at nine o'clock on the evening of 5 June. As it approached Wolverton Station, Constable Fossey, the policeman on duty, signalled that all was clear. The train then turned off into a siding instead of continuing on the main line. There it crashed into a line of laden coal trucks. The fifth and sixth carriages were smashed to pieces and the passengers were strewn around the line amongst the wreckage. The engine and the other carriages were mainly undamaged.

There were seven fatalities, all from the sixth carriage, which was Second Class. The report on the accident in *The Times* stated that unusually in such a collision the bodies seemed hardly injured and it was believed they all died from the shock of the sudden impact. The driver and fireman had jumped off the engine and survived.

It was stated that Constable Fossey had, after giving the all-clear signal, run to the points and moved them so that the mail train would run onto the siding. He claimed that he thought it was not the mail train but a luggage train. This seemed strange to the superintendent at the station, who had Fossey taken into custody.

There was a report of the accident in *The Morning Chronicle* of 8 June. Rather than go into details of the accident the newspaper published a list of the dead and injured. According to the report this was to relieve the anxiety of those who had family and friends travelling on the railway. No doubt it did set some people's minds at rest if their friends and family were not mentioned, although they did not seem to consider how the acquaintances of the dead and injured would feel on reading of the deaths in the newspaper. On 11 June *The Liverpool Mercury* performed a similar public service. They also printed a list of the dead and injured to relieve the anxiety of friends and family.

There was to be another serious accident on the London and North Western line a few months later. This one occurred at Winsford, near Hartford, on 9 November 1847. The collision involved a luggage train from Liverpool to Birmingham. As it reached Winsford a coal train came out of the sidings and both trains ran into each other. There were reports of a number of fatalities but it turned out that only the driver of the luggage train died. The fireman was injured, but not seriously.

A serious accident on the GWR occurred on 10 May 1848, involving the express train from Exeter as it passed through Shrivenham Station near Swindon. The train was late because of a problem on the South Devon line and taking on two extra carriages at Bristol, where there is a curve in the line before the station, giving the approaching driver a short view of the station.

In the goods shed at the station a truck was being unloaded by porters. To do this they had to move an empty horsebox and cattle truck out of the way. These were then moved out onto the main line. Due to the bend in the track the driver of the approaching express could not see the obstruction until it was too late.

The horsebox was destroyed but the cattle truck jammed against the platform and hit the luggage car behind the engine, which crushed the following carriages, including one Second Class carriage that contained thirty passengers. They were either thrown out or caught in the wreckage. The engine and part of the train, however, carried on going and was stopped further down the line.

The area around the station was described as being strewn with bodies and the injured. The station clerk, Mr Hudson, began to administer water to the survivors and shortly afterwards villagers from nearby arrived to help. There were only four dead but many others were injured.

During the inquest the men who had been unloading the goods wagon and who had moved the trucks onto the line stated that no one had told them that the express train had not yet passed through the station. The station clerk explained it was normal for the porters to move trucks around the station without orders to do so. He then said it was the policeman's job to make sure that the way was clear for trains, so he should have seen the trucks on the line.

There was some discrepancy in the policeman's evidence. He gave the all-clear to the train because he said the line was clear. He then saw the truck on the line, which, he said, must have just been moved there. The porter claimed it had been there for at least four minutes before the train struck it.

The coroner considered the evidence and whether the porters or the policeman were responsible for the accident. The jury returned a verdict of manslaughter against the two porters, James Weybury and William Willoughby. They were committed to Bedford Jail to await their trial. This must have been one of the few fatal accidents where someone was actually found to be responsible.

Whether this was the correct person, or persons, is another matter. *The Times* also had doubts upon this when on 13 May they published a story on the findings. They asked whether the station clerk, Mr Hudson, knowing that the express had not passed, should have mentioned this to the rest of the men at the station – especially Weybury, who had left the station for his dinner break and did not return until five minutes past three, five minutes after the express would normally have passed.

What about the policeman's evidence? There seems to be some dispute about how long the trucks had been on the line before he signalled that the line was clear. According to Weybury, it was four minutes. There was another statement by a witness, Joshua Moss, who had been standing on the platform. He saw the porters push the horsebox onto the line. They then fetched a cattle truck and put it against the horsebox. That would seem to have taken at least a few minutes.

Could the statement of the policeman then have been true in that he claimed that one moment they had not been there and then they were? Could it have been that those at the bottom of the employment ladder were the most likely to be apportioned the blame?

There was further evidence on this subject when it was reported in *The Morning Chronicle* of 15 May. It said that Michael Lane, a railway engineer, and Captain Symonds performed an experiment to see how long it would take to bring the horsebox and truck onto the line. It took them seven minutes, which seems to disprove the policeman's evidence.

There was another accident on the London and North Western Railway on 2 September 1848 at Newton Bridge, near Crewe. The express train from Liverpool was twenty minutes late at Wolverhampton and so was travelling faster than normal after this to catch up. The train was a small one with a tender, three carriages and a luggage van. A passenger later said that the train was shaking so much that they could barely stay in their seats. Just before Newton Bridge the engine came off the rails and sank into the embankment. The carriages were mainly on their sides.

Shortly after the accident a pilot engine was sent out from Birmingham to find out what had happened to the express. It drove straight into the luggage van, which had been thrown onto the other line, and then went into a ditch.

Surprisingly, there were no fatalities at the time of the accident. The passengers who were injured appeared to have nothing seriously wrong with them. However, there was later a death when Lieutenant Colonel Baird, who had been a passenger, died from the shock of the accident.

Working on the track was possibly an even more risky enterprise than travelling on the train as a passenger. We have already seen how a man was killed working in a tunnel when two trains passed through at the same time. A similar accident occurred at Hatherley Bridge, near Cheltenham, in September 1848. The victims were among a group of twenty men laying ballast on the line used by the GWR and the Bristol and Birmingham Railway.

A luggage train approached from Cheltenham and the men moved out of the way. Some got off the line and the others stood between the two lines. Then a passenger train came from the other direction and ran over three of the men, killing them instantly. Two others were badly injured.

The men had not been given a timetable but there was a boy who rang a bell when a train approached. Because of the noise of the luggage train no one heard the bell or the approaching passenger train. The driver of the passenger train had put his brakes on but due to a bend in the line he did not see the men until it was too late.

There was a strange story in *The Times* on 23 September 1848 concerning an accident at Wootton Basset Station on the GWR. The policeman who had been on duty at the station was in custody, which made the affair seem quite suspicious. There were no fatalities but there were a number of injuries.

A cheap excursion train, which had become popular on the GWR and some other lines, was due to travel from Bristol to Paddington and back. The train was fully booked with trippers eager to visit London. There were so many customers that eventually two trains were needed. One was to leave from Bath and the other from Bristol.

On the return journey the Bristol train arrived back safely. The Bath train reached Swindon safely but just after Wootton Basset Station there was a loud crash as the train hit a horsebox, which had appeared in the time between the first train passing and the second train arriving at that spot. The engine and four carriages fell down the embankment and into a field. The coupling to the remaining carriages had broken, leaving them on the line.

Because the first carriage fell on its side the passengers were trapped. There were doors only on one side and this side was facing the ground. This was a First Class carriage as Second and Third Class carriages tended to be open at the sides or even have no roof. The roof of the carriage had to be broken open with a sledgehammer to release the trapped passengers.

Mr Burton, the superintendent of the GWR police, was in one of these carriages but managed to climb out. One of the worst injuries was to the wife of the high bailiff of Bath; she was concussed. There were also other important people hurt.

There were rumours that the horsebox had been placed on the line deliberately. After enquiries were made at Wootton Basset the policeman on duty was arrested. It seems that the siding where the horsebox had been pushed onto the line was under his control and he should have seen the obstruction.

The following day *The Times* reported that the policeman, William White, was up before the magistrate. It seems that the policeman on day duty had told him that everything was alright so he had not bothered to check if the wheels of the horsebox were scotched. White was found guilty of neglect of duty and was imprisoned for two months.

The case was very similar to the accident at Shrivenham, where the policeman should have ensured that the line was clear and didn't. In the Shrivenham case the accident was blamed on someone else. Was the policeman prosecuted in this case because there were so many important people involved?

There was a serious accident on the Caledonian Railway in February 1849. The Caledonian Railway began life in the early nineteenth century and survived until 1923, when it became part of the London, Midland and Scottish Railway.

The accident occurred on 10 February when a mail train left Carlisle heading north at 9.15 pm. The train had a First and Second Class carriage and a mixed one of First and Second Class. There were three horseboxes, with nine horses, all bound for Perth. There was also a First and Second Class carriage for Edinburgh and a horsebox for Beattock.

The train had only travelled about 4 miles and reached Rockcliffe Station when the engine and tender became detached from the train and went off the line. A number of the carriages, the mobile Post Office and a horsebox also came off the rails and toppled down the embankment, which was about 15 feet high. One of the Second Class carriages was smashed to pieces by the Post Office truck.

According to *The Daily News*, the Second Class carriage turned topsy turvy and shivered to atoms. The driver and fireman were unhurt and began to search the train, which had been much busier than usual. Four dead were found under the Second Class carriage and another person, who was seriously hurt, was also found. The bodies and a number of other passengers were boarded onto a luggage train going back to Carlisle that was passing the site of the accident shortly after it happened. The injured man died during the night.

It is astonishing that the reason given in *The Times* for the accident was that the Second Class carriage, which was from the London and North Western Railway, was of the wrong gauge. In addition to the human casualties, six of the horses had to be destroyed.

The Glasgow Herald gave a different version. According to their report the accident was caused by a broken axle on a truck owned by the Lancaster and Carlisle Railway that had been attached to the train. Supposedly, the Caledonian Railway checked all the trucks on their trains twice before they left but the carriage that had failed wasn't theirs.

The Board of Trade Report on the accident was compiled by Captain J.L.A. Simmons Royal Engineers. He reported that the Second Class carriage, where the fatalities occurred, was at the bottom of the slope of the embankment. It was upside down underneath the Post Office carriage. The report included a diagram of the position of the carriages. Simmons stated that the wheels on some carriages may not have been fitted correctly. The man who had fitted some of them had already been dismissed for another case where the wheels had not been fitted correctly. Simmons also mentioned that similar axles had caused accidents in France. There was a diagram of the wheel on the axle and he suggested that a collar be fitted inside the wheel to stop movement and the wheel slipping inwards.

CHAPTER 5

1850 to 1860

There was a serious accident on 1 August 1850 on the Edinburgh and Glasgow Railway (the company was absorbed into the Northern British Railway in 1865). The accident involved a collision near Cowlairs Station and there were five deaths and many injuries.

There was a special train from Perth to take people to the Highland Society Exhibition in Glasgow. At Greenhill Junction the train was divided into two. One part went on to Cowlairs and was waiting for another train to pass when the second part of the special arrived and ran into the back of the first half.

According to *The Times*'s report on 2 August, two cattle trucks were smashed to pieces but for some reason these trucks were carrying twenty to thirty people. Although some carriages were quite primitive at this time it is the first time I have heard of cattle trucks being used for passengers.

The following day's report not only confirmed that cattle trucks were being used but that each of the two trucks held twenty-five to thirty people. Many of them had jumped before the collision occurred and were unhurt. It seems that the cattle trucks had no buffers and so were completely smashed. There were three deaths at the time of the accident and two more people died later.

There appeared to be a shortage of reports of the accident in other newspapers. Perhaps this was because it had occurred in Scotland. It *was* mentioned in the *Lancaster Gazette* on 3 August, which called the train 'a monster train of forty-one carriages'.

April 1851 was to see an accident on the short-lived Birkenhead, Lancashire and Cheshire Railway. (The railway's name was shortened to the Birkenhead Railway in 1859 and the following year it was taken over by the London and North Western Railway.)

The accident took place at Sutton Tunnel on 30 April. The line had been very busy due to the Chester Races. Three trains left Chester on the evening of the 30th. The first was too heavy for the engine and came to a stop in the

Sutton Tunnel, which is 1½ miles in length. This was then hit by the second train, which was unaware of the first being in the tunnel. There was little damage done by this collision. The third train then came along at a rapid speed and hit the second train, whose rear lights had been obscured by the steam in the tunnel. Being stuck in a long tunnel must have already been unpleasant, what with smoke and steam from the engines, especially in what were often open carriages. One can only imagine the scene once the second collision occurred.

A witness to the accident was Colonel Petit of the 50th Regiment. He was in the First Class carriage of the first train, which was at the end of the train. He said that the guard had been sent back to show a light but this had not prevented the collisions. The carriage he was in was crushed and he lost consciousness. He came round later and got out of the wreckage into the tunnel. It was very dark but he saw four or five dead passengers. The total number of dead was eight. One of the dead was a Mrs Ridgeway, who had been in a carriage with her servants. It was strange then that *The Morning Post* should say on 2 May only that three men of a 'humble sphere of life' were killed. There were also many people injured.

Another witness said that the carriages in the first train had no lights so this and the fact that they were in a tunnel must have made the situation worse. He also said that the third train had many open carriages in which people were standing up.

The witness reports did not seem to distinguish between the first collision and the second. It was said that the second train was going so slow that the collision caused no injuries so many passengers may not have been aware there had been two collisions.

One other witness, who was brought to the Albion Hotel in Manchester and who was injured, said that after the accident there was the greatest confusion on account of the utter darkness. There were many cries of help and people seeking wives, husbands and friends running about in the tunnel.

The Liverpool Mercury designated the accident the most serious for a considerable period. Despite the newspaper having a reporter on the spot they claimed that it was impossible to get any authoritative information.

The next fatal accident was to take place much further south, on the Brighton Railway. The building of the railway had begun in 1838. There had been a number of disagreements as to the best route that would avoid tunnels and gradients.

The accident involved a train from Brighton to Lewes. The train was small, consisting of a First, Second and Third Class carriages. There were two First

Class, three Second Class and four Third Class passengers on the train. Three of the five dead were from the Third Class carriage.

Halfway between Brighton and Lewes is the Falmer Tunnel, which is about 100 yards in length. On the Lewes side of the tunnel there is a steep slope and a number of bends. Drivers were warned not to exceed 20 miles an hour on these steep bends. It was suggested, however, that this speed limit was often ignored. It seems that the driver was not to blame as he was keeping to the normal speed. It was claimed that a sleeper had been placed on the line, causing the train to become derailed. This was according to the statement of a railway labourer who had seen three sleepers by the track but after the accident only saw two.

The driver survived the crash but had both legs amputated and later died. The fireman also died and the report in *The Times* mentioned that his father had been killed eighteen months earlier while working for the Brighton Railway Company at New Cross.

The inquest took place at the County Hall, Lewes before Mr F. Gells. There was unusually a jury of fifteen instead of twelve, although this was apparently normal in cases requiring investigation.

The *Hampshire Telegraph* of 7 June said that the Chief of Brighton Police, Mr Chase, had tried to find out if the accident was due to the malignant act of any individual.

The inquest concluded that the sleeper had been placed on the line as it was found splintered where the engine had struck it. The question was, who had put it there? There were suspicions on a young boy of ten who lived nearby. He was put in the witness box but cried before he could be questioned.

In a further story on 10 June in *The Times* it was suggested that the boy, James Boakes, had admitted placing the sleeper on the line but when the inquest restarted a few days later, he denied it. Eventually the verdict of the inquiry was that the deaths were due to the train hitting a sleeper but there was no proof as to who put it there.

The next fatal accident to occur was also in the south of the country. It took place on the Buckinghamshire Railway on 6 September 1851. The Buckinghamshire Railway was another short-lived company. It had begun operations in 1850 and became part of the London and North Western Railway in 1879.

The accident occurred at Bicester Station when an engine ran off the line while crossing some points, causing the carriages to turn over. The first report stated that a soldier, three children and a woman were killed, although it turned out that six people had died.

The reports of the accident in most newspapers were amazingly similar. All of them mentioned that the train was being pulled by one of Stephenson's six-wheeled patent engines. It would be difficult not to believe that either the same person wrote all of these reports or that they were all copied from one report.

There were some remarkably conflicting stories relating to the victims in later reports. One man was apparently pronounced dead and had been moved with the other dead bodies, who had all been railway labourers. Then warm bottles were placed on his feet and he came round. Another man, Joseph Locket, was unconscious. Surgeons from Oxford had arrived and decided to try trephining on Locket. This involved drilling a hole in the skull. Unfortunately it was unsuccessful and the patient died.

The Morning Chronicle of 9 September mentioned the 'excitement occasioned for miles around is intense in painful character by the arrival of the families of the victims.'

On 23 November 1851 there was another death on the London and North Western Railway, when the train from Rugby to London arrived at Weedon and was hit by a cattle train. First reports did not mention any deaths but this became evident later. There were, however, a large number of injuries.

The train had arrived at the station only to find a coal train on the line. There were no sidings at the station so the coal train had to be moved to the down line to allow the passenger train to pass. The train moved to the platform while the coal train was still moving across to the other line. Then the cattle train arrived and drove straight into the train at the platform.

One of the passengers was Captain Huish, the general manager of the railway company. At the moment of the collision he was standing with his head through the window speaking to someone on the platform. The collision caused him to hit his head on the side of the window.

There was, apparently, a policeman half a mile up the line to stop any trains coming into the station. There were also signals to stop any trains coming. The driver of the cattle train saw these but while reversing his engine he got it out of gear and did not notice until it was too late.

A report in *The Times* the following day, 25 November, announced that one of the passengers, a Mr Currie of Warrington, had died due to the head injuries he had received in the collision. The other injured were at the time doing well.

The reason for the collision was given as the engine on the cattle train being out of gear and unable to stop. The report went on to say that the driver had no right to be going so fast and he must have passed stop signals at least half a mile from the station. The government inspector of railways was likely to make an investigation as well as the one to be held by the coroner.

The following day there was a further report of the events during the coroner's inquest. The report mentioned there was little hope for the labourer from Northampton who had been dreadfully injured about the legs and thighs in the collision.

A fatal accident occurred on the London and North Western Line on 6 March 1852. There were three deaths due to this accident, which occurred near Kilburn Turnpike, where the Kilburn Omnibuses stopped. There was a coal depot close by and this was where the accident happened.

Five men were plate-lying on the line there when a down train passed them going through the tunnel. They moved onto the up line but at the same time a train to Euston approached in the other direction. Due to the noise of the first train and the men's attention being distracted by it, they did not notice the Euston train and three of them were run down. They were killed instantly and, according to the report, horribly mutilated due to being run over by several of the wheels. The labourers were just up from the country and had only been working there a few days. They were George Chapman, Richard Fenwick and William Rowley.

The inquest found that as well as the five men who were the opening gang, there were about sixty others close by. This large group had a policeman and an overlooker to warn the group of approaching trains. The opening group had neither.

The coroner was Mr Wakely MP, who said to the jury that he feared the regulations with respect to workmen on the lines were not sufficiently strict to ensure their safety. Despite this he went on to say that no blame was attached to anyone and accidental death was the verdict.

There was another fatal accident soon afterwards. This time it was on the London and South Western Railway. The L&SWR was one of the longer lasting railway companies. It began in 1838 and endured until the 1923 reorganization, when it became part of Southern Railways.

The accident occurred on 13 March and involved the down mail train that left Waterloo at 8.30 pm. The train consisted of the engine and tender, a guard's van, a Post Office tender, two Second Class and two First Class carriages. The accident happened about a mile before Bishopstoke when a tyre came off one of the engine wheels. The engine came off the line and fell down a 20-foot embankment. It took the guard's van and the Post Office tender with it. The fireman died instantly and the driver shortly afterwards at the Southampton Infirmary.

The year 1852 was not a good one as far as accidents were concerned. There was another fatal catastrophe on 12 July. This time it was on the Lancashire and Yorkshire Railway. The company was another that managed to last for some time, from its beginnings in 1848 right up until 1922.

The accident involved excursion trains taking Sunday school children and teachers from Burnley to York, Goole and Liverpool. It is surprising to think that people would risk taking large numbers of children on what might have then been considered quite a dangerous form of transport, although *The Morning Post* of 15 July seems to argue against this. It stated that it was remarkable how few accidents had hitherto occurred on what were called cheap trips or excursions. However, they went on to regret having to report an exception. The following day's *Daily News* explained that it was a Sunday school trip with the purpose of removing the children from the drunkenness experienced at the yearly Burnley Fair.

The Goole train was carrying Wesleyan Methodists and consisted of about thirty-five carriages. There were more than 1,000 passengers on board. The train had reached Goole and returned to Burnley at eleven thirty that evening. There was an unusual system at Burnley where the engine would be detached from the train, which was then run down onto the mainline, not usually used for passengers. The train instead ran down onto the normal passenger line, which had only a short platform ending in a stone wall. The train hit the buffers on the wall and two of the carriages were thrown upwards. As well as the injured there were hundreds of people on the station and it took some time to sort out the situation. It was a miracle that only four were dead but there was a large number of injured.

There was an investigation by Mr Hall, the passenger superintendent. He found that if the points been properly attended to the accident would not have happened. John Parker, the pointsman, was then taken into custody.

The Board of Trade report was written by Captain George Wynne, Royal Engineers. He criticized the employment of a stranger for important duties, such as when a porter took over the guard's duties. He said that this could happen regularly without superiors knowing about it. According to the report the station was under the control of a porter at the time of the accident. He also found that the train involved had buffers but because the train was made up of different carriages, some of these were 9 inches higher than the buffers on an adjoining carriage.

'Another fatal accident on the London and North Western Line' was a headline in *The Times* on 6 August 1852. It seems that around this time there were a number of accidents on the lines that belonged to this company.

There were quite a number of accidents on the LNWR, although similar numbers of accidents occurred on the lines of many other companies too, including the London and North Western, so the headlines in *The Times* suggesting there were more accidents on the LNWR seems a bit unfair. Perhaps it was just that some of these accidents occurred close together. Many of the other companies had around four to five fatal accidents from the early years of the railways up to the end of the nineteenth century.

The headline in *The Times* wasn't the first of this nature. *The Morning Chronicle* of 19 August 1848 had published a similar one: 'Another accident on the London and North Western Railway'. It is no surprise then that by the time of *The Times*'s headline, questions were being asked about the London and North Western Railway Company.

The first accounts of the 1852 accident did not report it as having been a fatal one. This only became evident later. The newspaper reported on the accident that took place on the LNWR line at the beginning of August and the investigation that took place at Coventry a few days afterwards. There had already been a report in *The Morning Chronicle* saying that the accident had been caused by the ash pan, which had fallen off the engine, causing the carriages to be derailed and go onto the other line, where they were hit by another train.

When investigations were held in front of juries, members of the jury were often told to ignore newspaper reports about the incidents. This investigation took place under the coroner W.H. Seymour, to investigate the death of 11-year-old William Floyd, one of the accident's victims. The railway company was represented by Mr Bruyeres, superintendent of the southern division, Mr O'Connell, chief of the locomotive department, and Superintendent Bedford of the railway police. The proceedings were also overseen by Mr Barr, one of the company's solicitors. The victims were represented by the Alderman of the Borough of Coventry, Mr Whitten.

The coroner showed some regard to the feelings of the company when he stated that in all the cases of this nature he had presided over, he had received every possible assistance from the railway authorities. Mr Bedford said that the directors of the company had instructed him to place the resources of the company at the disposal of any officer executing a public enquiry.

The driver of the 9.15 from Birmingham to London, which was involved in the accident, said the train appeared to be in order when they had left the station. As the train approached Bradwell Marsh the engine began to shake. He looked round to see that the engine had broken loose from the rest of the train and the carriages had gone across the down line. Within seconds the

An illustration by Frederick Talbot for an article in *The Harmondsworth Magazine* in 1898 showing an accident at Heathfield, where the engine went over an embankment.

Leamington train coming from the other direction smashed into the carriages. The driver went on to explain that on examining the engine he found that the ash box under the firebox was missing. It was later found on the tracks close to where the carriages had become derailed. The carriages had apparently hit the ash box and this had caused the derailment.

The driver thought the ash box must have hit something on the line that had caused it to fall off. He had not, however, felt the engine hit anything before the accident and nothing that could have caused this had been found on the line.

Mr Bedford informed the coroner that the locomotive foreman of Rugby and Birmingham, whose job it was to examine engines before they left the station, agreed with this version of events. The foreman, Abraham Marshall, stated that he had examined the engine before it had left and the ash pan had been secure, as had every other part of the engine. The coroner pointed out that the problem facing the jury was to decide if the ash pan had been knocked off or had fallen off. This was, of course, very hard to prove either way. Mr Whitten then stated that in the absence of positive proof, the cause of the accident could only be conjecture. He had, however, examined the ash pan and found that the bolts holding it on seemed to be worn away. This would explain why the driver of the engine had not felt any collision and why nothing had been found on the line. He thought that the ash box may have just fallen off due to its poor condition.

There was then some dispute when the representatives of the company argued that Mr Whitten was not a professional person and could not know whether the bolts had been worn. They claimed that any sign of wear would have led to repair.

A member of the jury asked if the ash box could be examined by an independent machinist that was resident in the town. A Mr Mosedale was then called, accompanied by the high constable of the borough.

Mr Mosedale went to Coventry Station and examined the ash box and the engine. He stated that one of the nibs that held the pan appeared to have been broken for some time and the others were in a very bad state. The ironwork of the pan was also in a bad state. This was in his opinion caused by wear and the fire in the engine. He thought that the pan had probably fallen off. He was unable to examine the ash box closely, however, as the engine was by then back in use and had a fire in the firebox.

The hearing was then adjourned until 11 August. The coroner told the jury that in the previous hearing some members of the jury had decided on their view without having heard all the evidence. No doubt he was referring to those who thought the ash pan had fallen off

At the new hearing it was revealed that the engine involved had been in an accident a month earlier, when it had turned over. It was also claimed that repairs had been carried out to the ash pan a short while before the accident. Normally all repairs were recorded in writing. For some unexplained reason there was no written record of these repairs having been carried out. It was stated that the repairs included some welding, which could have been faulty. An inspection of the ash pan before the train left would, however, not have been able to recognize that the weld may have been defective. This would then seem to excuse the fact that the ash pan may have fallen off due to poor condition, which might not have been apparent with a cursory inspection.

The hearing was once again adjourned and restarted on 25 August, when a verdict was finally reached. It was stated that the three deaths that occurred in the accident were due to the ash pan falling off the train, but there was no evidence to prove what had caused this.

It is no surprise then that there should be some reaction in the press when, a few days after the previous accident, another fatal accident took place on the lines of the London and North Western Railway. This occurred on 5 August 1852. The 9.30 express from Liverpool had left at its normal time. It had twelve carriages and two brake vans. When it reached Crewe at 10.45 an additional engine was attached to assist the train up the Madeley Bank, which was a steep slope. The extra engine would then detach itself when the train was back on level ground. This took place and the engine went off in front of the train by increasing its speed. It seems that when the train passed Whitmore it came round a sharp bend and found the engine stationary on the line as it was attempting to cross onto the down line. There was no chance of stopping the train and it crashed into the stationary engine. The driver of the express was killed instantly.

The engine attached to the train turned completely round and destroyed the stationary engine. Eight of the carriages were thrown off the line and overturned. Although there were a number of injuries, there were no other casualties.

Another fatal crash occurred on the GWR in November 1852, which seems to have been caused by a number of reasons. A train from Birmingham to London had reached Hayford Station late due to a number of slips along the line because of heavy rain. The train was to pick up a goods wagon at the station that was on the other side of the rails. This meant that the train would have to cross the down line. When the train was halfway across, the express from Paddington to Birmingham was heard approaching. The express was not supposed to stop at the station. The driver of the London train tried to move out of the way but according to the report the wet rails made it difficult for him to get away quickly enough. The express from London then hit the engine of the other train.

Surprisingly when one considers the speed at which the express must have been travelling, there was only one fatality. This was George Thompson, the driver of the express. His death was not due to the collision, however, as his body was found some distance away. It is believed that he jumped from the engine before the trains collided and this led to his death. The fireman, who stayed on the engine, survived.

Some blame was attached to the stationmaster for allowing the train to cross the line when the express was due. There were discretionary powers available to the master to allow this and the danger signals had been displayed to warn the express driver. It is believed that he must not have seen them.

There was some doubt about this view of events at the inquest on Thompson, which took place at the Red Lion Tavern in Heyford under Mr J. Churchill, the county coroner, and was attended by Mr Tyrell, the chief superintendent of the GWR. The jury found that Thompson's death was accidental due to his throwing himself against a scotch on the line – a timber wedge used to keep points locked open or closed.

The jury then added their opinion that moving another train across the line without raising the danger signal was contrary to the rules and regulations of the company and that great culpability, neglect and want of judgement should be attached to the stationmaster for allowing the train to be moved when the express was due. There was no mention of any consequences for the stationmaster.

The final fatal accident of 1852 took place a few days before Christmas. It was on the London and North Western Line and occurred just before Harrow. The up express train was driven off the line and the guard of the brake van next to the engine was killed. The front wheel of the engine had come off the line but the rear driving wheel held it on for 400 yards. One of the wheels lost a tyre and the engine came off the line to the left. The guard's van was on the line but the weight of the train pushed it off to the left, smashing it to pieces, as well as the man inside.

The year 1853 began as the last year had finished, with an accident on 3 January that *The Times* called the most terrible for many years. It was on the London and North Western again, so perhaps *The Times's* headlines were not as exaggerated as I have previously suggested.

The accident happened about a mile from Oxford and the first reports detailed seven deaths, although this was expected to rise. The disaster took place as two trains coming from opposite directions collided. The incident came about because the Wolvercote Tunnel was undergoing repairs after having suffered a collapse. While repairs were being carried out there was only a single line in use between Oxford and Wolvercote. On the day of the accident a passenger train was waiting at Oxford for a coal train to pass in the opposite direction. It was only a small train, with one carriage of each class. The stationmaster had told the driver to wait until the coal train passed.

While waiting, an engine came through the station with no train. It had a white light on the front. Coal trains carried a blue light. The driver of the passenger train set off as soon as the engine had passed. The stationmaster had by then retired to his office. The guard realized that it was not the coal train that had passed and put on the brakes. The fireman and driver either ignored this or did not see the signal from the guard to stop.

It was reported that the driver of the passenger train was going very fast despite instructions to go slowly on this stretch of line. He did not appear to try and stop when the coal train with two engines came in sight. Although the people in the station had tried to stop the train leaving the station, the policeman on the bridge just outside the station had changed the signal to green.

According to Talbot's article in *The Harmondsworth Magazine*, although only the engine driver died in this accident at Heathfield, it cost the railway company £13,000 in compensation.

A fatal accident that took place on 24 February 1853 was unusual in that the victim was a director of the GWR. There were four directors of the company on the morning express from Bristol to London on their way to the weekly board meeting. The train had just reached Ealing when the porter that accompanied express trains and the driver noticed that one of the three First Class carriages was off the rails. The driver applied the brakes but as he did so the couplings between the First and Second Class carriages broke free. The First Class carriages being at the rear of the train then ran up the embankment. The first carriage then turned over, crushing the other two.

The second carriage was the most seriously damaged and this had been where the four directors were sitting. They were Richard Potter of Gloucester, Henry Simmons of Reading, Doctor Richard Smith also of Reading, and James Gibbs of Clifton. It was Gibbs who was killed instantly. Doctor Smith was injured but the other two men were unhurt. No one else in the second carriage suffered more than superficial injuries.

It seems that Mr Gibbs, despite being a director of a railway company, had little faith in the safety of the means of travel. A few weeks before he was killed he had taken out an insurance policy against dying in a rail accident.

In the carriage that turned over, one man, Adam Duff of Reading, was found to have his head stuck in the hole where a lamp normally was. The rescuers found it very difficult to free him. His only injuries were broken fingers.

The official report of the accident stated that it was caused by a breakage of one of the scroll irons or spring hangers that are attached to the leading wheel of the carriage. The result of this would be to give the axle box free reign and lead to it coming off the rails.

The eminence of the victim led to some differences at the inquest, which was held under Mr Wakely at the Feathers Inn next to Ealing Station. It was attended by Captain Wynn, the government inspector of railways. An interesting comment from Mr Wakely was that in the twelve years that he had been a coroner, and despite the large number of railway lines in his district, this was the first inquest he had conducted on a First Class passenger. There had been four or five on Second and Third Class passengers. In his view it was the cushions in First Class carriages that made them safer and it was a pity that steps could not be taken to render other classes of carriages as safe.

It seemed as though not only had the new year begun as badly as the previous one had ended, but it was on course to beat it for the number of accidents. The third fatal accident of the year occurred on 4 March on the Lancashire and Yorkshire Railway at Dixon Fold Station near Manchester. The first reports mentioned three killed but this was to rise to six. The train involved was an express, with three carriages from Edinburgh and two from Liverpool. It passed the station at between 40 and 50 miles an hour. After the station there were a number of curves on the line. Passengers said afterwards that the carriages were swaying from side to side before the accident. The engine then left the line and turned across the rails, smashing the three following coaches to pieces.

The driver was dead, as was another man who was on the engine on his way to work in Manchester. The fireman survived. One woman found herself lying across the line when she came round. She crawled off the line despite being badly hurt and got to the embankment, where she found one of her children, a 5-year-old boy, who was dead. She lay there for hours unable to move before help finally reached her. The railway company were criticized for the time it had taken for help to reach the site. One man who had severe head injuries had to walk 6 miles to find help.

There were a few months without any serious accidents, until 4 October 1853. The accidents that then occurred made up for the brief remission. The accident was due to a collision on the Midland Railway, where an engine had come off the line. Help was sent from Derby but there were not enough men, so another engine with more men was sent. The men in the first engine had by this time got the derailed engine back on the line and were returning to Ambergate on the same line when the second engine came along and they collided. There were several injuries but no deaths. Despite this, *The Morning*

Chronicle of 6 October described it as having fatal and disastrous consequences.

Another accident occurred the following day at Straffen, in Ireland, on the Great Southern and Western Railway. The company was one of the largest railways in Ireland and had taken over many smaller companies. It also had the biggest gauge railway in the country.

The accident took place a few miles from Dublin. A passenger train had stopped on the line between Sallins and Straffen due to a problem with the engine. One of the company's solicitors was on the train and he ordered someone to go back down the line with a signal as there was a cattle train following. Fifteen minutes later, the light of the cattle train appeared on the line. Many of the people who had got out of the passenger train got back in thinking that the train might now move and the cattle train must be going slowly due to the warning it had been given. The cattle train then ran into them at full speed.

The First Class carriage at the rear of the train was completely destroyed. The rest of the carriages were piled onto each other and one of them broke apart. One of the sadder stories was of an English gentleman who was travelling with his sister, his wife and their baby. They had been outside the train speaking to another gentleman as the train approached. The women got back on with the baby. The gentleman waited while the man he was talking to, a Mr Jelly, climbed into the carriage. The ladies then wanted to get back out as the cattle train approached. The Englishman told them to stay there as he was about to get in as well when Mr Jelly was out of the doorway. The train then hit and Mr Jelly was decapitated and his legs were cut off. The two women were also killed, although the baby survived. The final death toll was eighteen.

It was around this time, in September 1854, that *The Bristol Mercury* reported on a case of money being obtained under false pretences that related to the railways. However, the report had little interest in the crime and more in the accused – Elizabeth Ann Holman, who was dressed as a railway labourer. She was described as very boyish looking with her hair cut short. Holman was twenty-three and the daughter of a retired pay sergeant of the 43rd Regiment. She had dressed as a boy since she was thirteen and after working as a farm labourer had gained employment with the Cornwall and Tavistock Railway, filling barrows with earth.

Her workmates were apparently aware that Holman was a woman and they called her Lizzie. She had been living with a man named Pearce and had two children. One of them had died and the other lived with her sister. She claimed that she would dress as a man until she was transported for it.

There was, after the bad years of 1852 and 1853, almost two years without a serious accident, until 12 September 1855, when another fatal crash occurred. This was at Reading on the London and South Eastern Railway and it left seven people dead.

The first reports gave the number of fatalities as four, although *The Standard* said that three had died and many more were so seriously injured that their lives were despaired of. This report also went on to explain how a Mr Sowden had his arms and legs cut off. It also mentioned how he was a highly respected resident of Reading. *The Daily News* of 14 September stated that three passengers and a servant of the railway had died. It also reported that one man was to blame for the accident but he was one of the dead so could not explain what had been the cause.

It seems that a telegraphic message was received at Reading asking for an engine to take a train along the Reigate Line to Reading. An engine was sent, driven by Joseph Crossley. The driver was described as a good man. For some reason he did not take the engine straight away and when he did arrive he did not speak to anyone but went and took the engine out of the shed. He did not even light the lamps, despite being reminded by the man who was acting as his fireman.

The engine left at 7.15 am, although it was known that a train was due at the station at 7.35. The train would be on the same line as the engine. The fireman said that both he and the driver were aware that the train was due but were not aware that they were on the same line. About a mile from Reading, at Hathaway's Farm, the engine hit the oncoming train. The train had only two carriages, a First and a mixed First and Second Class. The engines were both destroyed, as was the mixed carriage. Crossley was one of the dead, found with an oil can in his hand. The other dead mentioned at the time were all passengers.

The inquest was held at the public offices in Reading, under Mr Blandy. The general manager, Mr Barlow, represented the railway company. The first actions of the jury were to examine the bodies, which is what normally happened. Jesse Ferguson was interviewed. He was a cleaner who had been getting the engine ready for Crossley. When there was no fireman the man who cleaned the engine would replace him. His job was to light the lamps, but he had been told not to by Crossley, who said they would light them at Wokingham. Ferguson also explained that in the absence of a pointsman the driver would order the fireman to set the points, but Crossley had not done this.

James Wallace, the foreman porter at Reading, said he saw Crossley drive the engine out of the shed and onto the down line. He was going about 15 to 20 miles an hour. All the danger signals were up but were ignored by the driver. Wallace then said that if a switchman had been at his post he could have not done anything as Crossley was going too fast to change lines. Wallace had expected the engine to reverse onto the turntable.

It was agreed that Joseph Crossley was guilty of manslaughter in regard to the dead. It was also agreed that he killed himself. The jury then suggested that a switchman should be permanently on duty at the signals and points connected to a station.

With the new regulations introduced with Lord Campbell's Act claims for compensation by injured passengers were becoming more common. There was a claim for compensation in Scotland in December 1856. Mr William Dobie, an ensign in the 79th Regiment, was claiming £2,000 in damages due to a badly broken leg sustained in a railway crash at Cove Station in July 1855.

Dobie claimed that his military career had been ruined due to the permanent damage to his leg and that if it hadn't been for the injury he could have risen to a high level in the army. The Aberdeen Railway Company did not contest that the accident had been their fault but they did contest the severity of the injuries. It was agreed that Dobie would never recover to an extent that would allow him to continue his military career and he was awarded £950.

By this time, safety standards did seem to be improving, with fatal accidents now occurring every few years rather than every few months. It was not until the 28 June 1858 that another fatal accident occurred. It was on the North Kent Railway near Lewisham Station. According to *The Morning Post* of 29 June, the dreadful accident occurred at a late hour. It gave no number of fatalities but said that forty were seriously injured. Although fatal accidents were becoming rarer the number of fatalities seemed to be increasing. *The Daily News* of 30 June reported that eleven were dead as a result of the frightful accident at Lewisham, where also many were so seriously injured to render their recovery almost hopeless. The majority of the dead were in the last carriage of what had been a stationary train, which was an open, Third Class type.

An up train had stopped just before Lewisham Station when a train from Maidstone came up and crashed into it. The brake van of the Maidstone train was wedged onto one of the carriages, stopping the passengers from getting out. *The Daily News* report went on to say that the stationary train had no light and that no signals were set to warn of the train's presence.

The report in the following day's *The Times* went into more detail. It stated that it was common for trains to run at short intervals and the line in question was covered by Tyler's electric signal system. This supposedly meant that the stationmaster at one station could not let another train through unless he had a telegraph message saying that the previous train has passed the next station.

The first train had stopped at the signal just before the station and the guard was sent back to warn the next train. The superintendent of the railway held a brief investigation and felt it was his duty to have the driver and fireman of the second train taken into custody. By driving through a danger signal they had neglected their duty. The guard who had been sent back said that he had waved his red lamp at the second train and blown his whistle. The train had continued on and passed him at about 20 miles an hour. He then heard the collision.

The report went on to say that the pointsman and the railway officials whose duty it was to attend the signals had been suspended. In addition to the inquest there would also be an inquiry under captain Wynne, Royal Engineers, for the Board of Trade.

There was another fatal accident the following year and again the number of fatalities was in double figures. Twelve people died, eleven of them at the time of the crash, which happened on 23 August 1858 on the Oxford and Worcester Railway between Round Oak and Brettel Lane stations.

The disaster was another Sunday school outing excursion, this one to Worcester from Wolverhampton. There were special return fares of one shilling for adults and sixpence for children. Due to its cheapness there were forty-five carriages carrying a total of nearly 2,000 passengers.

The Birmingham Daily Post stated that it was a special train that stopped at all stations from Wolverhampton to Worcester for the teachers and children of various schools. *The Morning Chronicle* of the same day printed the same article but credited it to *The Birmingham Daily Post* of the same day so it must have obtained and copied the article very quickly.

The Blackburn Standard of 25 August said that the accident was on the very cheap school excursion and was the most serious to occur on a railway in the Midland District. Eleven were killed instantly and another died over the next few hours. The recovery of the injured was despaired of and several victims would be maimed for life.

A decision had been made that, instead of a monster train with two engines that made the outward journey, there would be two trains with one engine each on the return. The first train left Worcester on the return journey at 6.25 pm. It had twenty-nine carriages. The second train left fifteen minutes later, with sixteen carriages. As the first train approached Round Oak Station, which was up a steep incline, twelve or thirteen coaches became detached due to a broken coupling. The guard in the rear brake van applied the brakes but this did little to stop the carriages, which gathered speed and ran into the second train. The worst effects were felt in the last two carriages of the runaway train and they were almost completely destroyed.

The report in *The Times* the following day stated that on the outward journey there had been two broken couplings on the train when it had comprised forty-five coaches and two engines. Luckily, this was when the train was going down an incline as there was another train following closely behind. It was due to these breakages that it had been decided to divide the train for the return journey.

CHAPTER 6

1860 to 1870

The year 1860 began quite well for the railways; the first serious accident did not happen until September. The incident happened on the Lancashire and Yorkshire Railway on 4 September near Helmshore Station and involved excursion trains returning from Manchester. *The Birmingham Daily Post* called it the 'most dreadful railway accident ever to occur in this area and perhaps in the kingdom'.

There had been three excursion trains from Colne, Burnley and Accrington to Manchester for the fête at Belle Vue Gardens. The three trains taking the trippers home left Manchester before 11.00 pm. The first arrived safely. The second, with eighteen carriages, reached Helmshore Station at about midnight.

The station is on top of a large incline, which stretches for about 4 miles. As the train tried to leave the station the couplings between the third and fourth carriages broke. Fifteen carriages then ran back down the incline and, at about 300 yards from the station, collided with the third train.

The casualties were confined to the loose carriages, especially in the two at the rear, which struck the engine of the third train. The third train had almost managed to come to a stop and the impetus was with the runaway carriages. There were eleven deaths and up to 100 injuries.

The inquest was held at the Turner's Arms Inn at Helmshore. It was overseen by Mr Hargreaves, the coroner for Blackburn. It was stated at the inquest that only ten people had died, not eleven. There seemed little to find as the accident was obviously due to the broken coupling.

The year 1860 was turning out to be a bad one after all with regard to fatal accidents. The next one took place on the Trent Valley Railway. The railway had been built in 1845 by an independent company but before it was completed it was taken over by the London and North Western Railway. In spite of this, when the accident occurred the company was still named in the newspapers as the Trent Valley Railway.

The accident occurred on 16 November near Atherstone Station. There were ten deaths – the toll reaching double figures being in keeping with all other recent fatal railway accidents.

The actual number of dead wasn't known straight away. *The Daily News* of 17 November stated in its headline that there was 'the loss of nine lives in a most deplorable and fatal accident'.

A cattle train from Holyrood had been on its way to Peterborough. At about two o'clock in the morning the train was shunting onto a siding to allow the Scottish mail train to pass. Before the cattle train cleared the line the mail train arrived travelling at speed and struck it. The last four trucks on the cattle train were destroyed. The mail train's engine was also wrecked and thrown off the line. As well as smashed carriages and injured people there were a number of dead cattle spread over the crash site. The ten human fatalities were mostly amongst the men who had been in charge of the cattle and were travelling in the rear truck of the cattle train. Thankfully the passengers on the mail train were unhurt apart from a few minor bruises. The fireman on the mail train was the only fatality from the passenger train. His body was found under the engine.

An early report in *The Times* stated that the accident was due to the driver of the mail train not having observed the signals. The danger signals were about a quarter of a mile down the line from the crash site. There had apparently been an act of gross negligence by either the engine driver for ignoring the signals or the signalman for not setting the danger signals.

At the inquest the driver of the mail train said that he only saw a danger signal about 100 yards before the spot where the train crashed, when it was too late to stop. The driver also said that normally he would be told at Tamworth if there was a train ahead. On this occasion he hadn't been informed.

The Board of Trade report was written by Colonel W. Yolland, who explained how the engine of the mail train went over the guard's van of the cattle train and the van next to it where the nine men died. Notices had been issued by the district supervisor to officials of several stations in the area about special cattle trains that were running. These notices did not seem to have been passed on to train drivers.

A report in *The Times* on 26 August 1861, on an accident that had taken place the previous day on the London and Brighton Railway, stated that it was the 'most terrible accident that has occurred since the introduction of the railway system', and it was no exaggeration.

This view was reiterated in other newspapers. *The Daily News* and *The*

Morning Post of 26 August also stated that they believed it was one of the most terrible accidents since the introduction of the railways. They both mentioned that the sensation was intensified because of where the accident took place. The two newspapers also published the same interview with Mr Hawkins, the traffic manager of the line. The accident resulted in twenty-three deaths, the most in any British railway accident so far.

Although there seemed to be similar or even word-for word-reports in different newspapers some did try to present their own exclusive angle on these stories. *The Morning Chronicle* of the same day gave information of the accident scene, which was in the second tunnel on the main line from Brighton – the longest on the line.

The accident occurred in the Clayton Tunnel about 5 miles from Brighton. *The Times* went on to say that three trains from Brighton to London left the station between 8.00 and 8.30 am. The first train went into the tunnel and a little later the second one approached. The signalman, knowing the first train had just entered the tunnel, signalled the second train to stop, which it did but only after it had entered the tunnel. It then began to reverse out again. At all tunnels there was a man stationed at each end.

The man at the tunnel entrance telegraphed the man at the exit to see if the train had left the tunnel, meaning the second train, and was told it had. It was, in fact, the first train that had left the tunnel; the second was still reversing out. The man at the entrance, thinking the tunnel was clear, signalled for the third train to enter the tunnel and then the two trains collided.

The engine of the third train hit the rear carriage of the second train, destroying it and then running over the top of it. The horror of what had happened must have been magnified by the fact that it occurred in the darkness of the tunnel. It would have been almost impossible for the passengers to see what was going on.

A special train arrived shortly afterwards with doctors and workmen to help. They found that many of the bodies were underneath the engine of the third train, finding at least twenty-two dead as soon as they arrived. The report went into very detailed information of some of the injuries suffered by the deceased.

The dead and injured were taken to Brighton. The dead were placed in the company library, where they were to await identification. The injured went to the Sussex County Hospital. Some of the injured had to have limbs amputated and one of them later died. A child of two, who was not badly injured, was thought to be the child of one of the dead.

Much of the front part of the train that had been reversing was undamaged and its passengers unhurt. The complete part of the train was uncoupled and went on to Hassocks Gate Station, where it was easier to check that the passengers were not hurt. This left only the worst part of the accident at the Brighton end of the tunnel to be dealt with.

The following day, *The Times* printed a list of the names of the dead. They also reported that none of the injured was expected to die. There had been a man whose leg had been amputated who had been expected to die but he had made a miraculous recovery overnight. The child was identified by her father, who came from London. He also identified his wife's body. The child was then described as very ill but there were faint hopes for its survival.

An inquest was held at the town hall in Brighton under David Black, the borough coroner. One of the deceased had still not been identified. The solicitor of the London and Brighton Railway, Mr Faithfull, and Mr Conningham MP, also attended. Connningham was one of the railway company's directors. A number of members of Parliament were closely connected with railway companies.

The seriousness of the accident and the number of deaths obviously stirred up a great deal of public interest. Articles on the disaster continued to appear in the newspapers for some time.

The next fatal accident on the railways was only a few days after the London to Brighton catastrophe and was also situated in the south of the country. It happened on the North London Railway.

The company had lines that ran from London to the docks along the Thames. In 1851 a new line had opened to Hampstead Road to join the London and North Western Line. The accident occurred on 2 September 1861 on the Hampstead Junction Line, which had only been open two years. It was used by those travelling to Kew and Richmond.

Involved was a special train running from Camden Town to Kew. The train had to pass a coal depot near Kentish Town Station. A coal train with nineteen trucks was crossing the main line when about halfway across it was struck by the passenger train, resulting in sixteen deaths. The engine and some of the passenger carriages then fell down the embankment.

The difference between this and other accidents was that most of them occurred some distance from London. As this happened in Kentish Town, *The Times* reported that news of it was known all over London very quickly. It also said that many people had friends and relatives who had gone to Kew for a day out and would be worried about whether they were on the train. This was compounded by the fact that trains coming back from Kew could not run until after midnight due to the line not being clear because of the accident.

There was some confusion as to the cause of the accident. This was made more complicated by the fact that the passenger train belonged to the North London Railway. The coal train belonged to the London and North Western Railway and the workers on the station in the area were employees of the L&NWR.

The Times said that the accident was similar to the previous one on the Brighton line and was due to signals. Although there was no tunnel involved this time there was a series of bends in the line that made visibility for any distance difficult.

The Bury and Norwich Post had a headline on 3 September that stated there had been 'another terrible railway accident – great loss of life'. The report described how after the accident occurred there were moans of the dying, cries of the wounded and the lamentations of those who missed their relatives.

The next accident occurred much further north than the previous two and was almost as serious. On 13 October 1862 sixteen people died and many were injured on the Edinburgh and Glasgow Railway. The accident involved a collision between a train from Glasgow and one from Edinburgh. The collision took place at Craigton Bridge, near Winchburg Station, about 12 miles east of Edinburgh. The line here runs along a deep cutting through solid rock with some tunnelling. The accident occurred on the open section. One line was under repair and the traffic was operating on the up line leading to Edinburgh.

The trains were both very busy and most of the passengers suffered some level of injury. It was thought the collision was due to the inexperience of a signalman. As well as the mistake putting them on the same line there was also a curve in the line, which meant that the drivers did not see each other's train until it was much too late. Both engines were seriously damaged and were forced back onto the following carriages. Although not being in a tunnel, as the accident happened in the cutting, which was about 20 feet deep, as it was almost evening it was very dark at the accident site.

There were eleven deaths at the scene. The other deaths occurred later at the hospitals where the injured were taken. Both firemen and the driver of the Edinburgh train died. There were some remarkable escapes, such as a man from the Waverley Temperance Hotels of London and Edinburgh, Mr Cranston, who was in the first carriage of the Glasgow train. As the collision happened he was sitting by the door. The side of the carriage fell away and he was rolled out onto the line. This was just as the engine landed on top of the carriage in which he had been sitting.

Another man was thrown against the breast of a woman sitting opposite him. The woman died instantly but the man lived. Not all were so lucky and the guard of the Glasgow train lost his wife and one of his children in the crash.

The final paragraph of *The Times*'s story stated that the death toll had reached seventeen as a commercial traveller from Birmingham had just died. It also mentioned that the signalman, George Newton, had been apprehended.

Although the number of fatalities occurring in railway accidents had risen over the past few years there had only been one serious accident per year. This pattern continued and the next one was on 3 August 1863. This was on the Lynn and Hunstanton Railway and resulted in seven deaths.

The railway had opened in 1862 and served the new seaside town of Hunstanton. There were regular trains carrying those who came to the seaside for a week as well as trains for day trippers. According to *The Times,* the line was much used by people from Lynn and the local towns. There had been heavy excursion trains throughout the season, with people attracted by cheap fares.

The accident was reported very quickly in *The Morning Post* the day after it had occurred, thanks to an electric telegraph sent about the accident, the readers were informed. *The Birmingham Daily Post* published their report the following day and had an exclusive angle on the accident. They told readers that the accident occurred only a few miles from the Norfolk seat of the Prince of Wales.

There were three trains that ran between nine in the morning and four in the afternoon. There were also excursions from Wisbech and Cambridge. The Lynn and Hunstanton return train was to leave at 7.45 pm. Due to the number of passengers two trains were made up and the second left fifteen minutes after the first.

The accident was rather unusual. The first train managed the journey but passed a bullock in a dyke next to the line. The second train also passed the bullock until one carriage reached it. This was a First Class carriage and so was wider than the previous ones. This was about half a mile past Wootten.

It seems that the First Class carriage hit the bullock and made it fall onto the line. The carriage then went off the line, taking with it two more carriages that were behind. The First Class passengers escaped unhurt. It's no surprise that there was also a Third Class carriage involved and that it was smashed to pieces. It was amongst the passengers in this carriage that the fatalities occurred.

The Times's report went on to say that railway accidents were quite new to the area. They believed that the East Anglian lines may have been, until this episode, entirely free from serious accidents. That may, of course, have been due to there not having been many railways in the area.

The inquest was opened at the Ship Inn, Gaywood. The coroner was Mr Thomas Martin Wilkin. After examining the bodies he said that there would be much discussion on the effectiveness of the fences in the nearby field. Cattle had been found on the line a number of times before. Horses had also been found on the line when a special train passed bringing a party of railway officials up after the accident.

There was another accident in the south of the country on 7 June 1864 and it involved another holiday excursion train – this one a train returning from the Ascot races on the South Western Railway. These unscheduled trains often seemed to be more at risk than the normal timetabled ones.

Many newspaper reports when discussing an accident would call it the worst to have occurred in the area. *The Morning Post* came up with another angle. The writer said that it was the most fearful accident that had ever attended the transmission of passengers to various race meetings. It was described in *The Times* as a long, unmanageable train packed with holidaymakers such as are only seen at race times. It was one of two similar trains that left the races at seven o'clock in the evening. The second supposedly left as soon as was safe after the first one.

There had been some difficulties at the races, with a number of false starts. This had led to problems for the railway company. They knew that they would have a rush of passengers as the races ended later than expected. This seems to be why the trains had followed each other so closely.

The first train stopped at Egham Station about an hour after it had left Ascot. There was some dispute at the station as complaints were made about card sharps being present in one of the carriages. There was disagreement over whether they should be removed and this delayed the train at the station.

The second train arrived just as the first began to move. It was so obvious that there was going to be a collision that those at the station told the passengers on the first train to jump off. The guard in the rear van already had. There was a collision and two carriages were destroyed. Five people died instantly. Two more died later and about twenty-five people were injured. The dead and injured were all on the first train. The second train was going fast and there had been no signals to warn it about the first.

Westminster Court heard the case of a man on 8 December who had claimed damages from the Great Eastern Railway for injuries he suffered in a railway accident. A doctor, who was the medical officer of a club the man had belonged to, acted for him and won his case. The doctor had then claimed twenty percent of his damages. The man was in court trying to claim this back. He had believed that as he was a member of the club the doctor had been acting for him without charge. He was successful in getting the money back.

The year 1864 was one of the worst for some time, with another accident on 16 December. This occurred on the North Kent Railway. This was also another accident that occurred in a tunnel – the Blackheath Tunnel – and involved a passenger and a goods train. *The Daily News* explained how this accident was similar to the one that had occurred in the Clayton Tunnel a few years before.

The fast train from Maidstone had left the station at 2.40 pm. It had stopped at Woolwich at a quarter past four. It was claimed that signals were set at clear at Charlton and at the entrance to the tunnel. The passenger train was travelling at about 40 miles per hour as it entered the tunnel. It then ran into a ballast train en route from Higham to London. The accident was unusual in that it was on the ballast train that most of the fatalities occurred.

Five platelayers on the ballast train were killed straight away. The passengers on the other train were thrown about and injured. The driver and fireman were badly scalded. Again due to the accident occurring in a tunnel, it took some time to get help to the injured.

It was later reported that part of the ballast train had become detached from the rest of it and had been left in the tunnel. The remainder of the train had carried on towards its destination seemingly unaware of the rest being left behind.

The Board of Trade Report was written by Captain H.W. Tyler. He said that the train in the tunnel was slipping due to wet tracks and that the fireman was applying sand to the rails. He also explained how the Blackheath signal box was being operated by a porter who had only worked train telegraph instruments a few times in the past year.

The man took charge of the instruments every third Sunday and a couple of other days a month, usually due to staff sickness. The report went on to explain how the man had got confused as to what was going on. Tyler also said that those working in signal boxes should have had the means of speaking to each other.

The date of 7 June was turning out to be unlucky. Seven people had died on the same day the previous year. On 7 June 1865, eleven people died on the Shrewsbury and Chester Railway. One of *The Times*'s Parliamentary reporters was a passenger on the train so the newspaper received an early and detailed report.

The accident again involved an excursion train. There were thirty-five carriages being pulled by two engines and it was very busy. It left Birkenhead just before 11.00 pm and was about twenty-five minutes late. It was delayed again at Chester for about thirty minutes.

The reporter said it was obvious that the driver was trying to make up for being late by the speed the train was travelling at after it left Chester. The line before Rednal had been subject to work, was supposedly unsettled and should have only been used slowly by the train. There was apparently no decrease in speed at all as the train travelled over the recently altered line. The train then began to shake and the engines came off the line. One engine went to the right and the other to the left, followed by First Class coaches.

It was interesting that *The Times*'s reporter said that one of the smashed carriages lay on the right of the train – the side where the doors of the carriages were locked. In the latter end of the train the doors were locked on both sides of the carriages and so the passengers had to climb out of the windows. This is the first report I have seen that mentioned carriage doors being locked.

The worst injuries and many of the deaths were amongst the First Class passengers. This included a number of children. There were eleven deaths and many of the bodies were seen by and described by *The Times*'s correspondent. It was then two hours before help arrived from Shrewsbury.

The Birmingham Daily Post began its report with a headline stating that thirteen were killed and upwards of thirty were injured. It then went on to concentrate on the local angle of the crash, which was the worst to have happened anywhere near Birmingham for some time. The accident also caused excitement in the town because there was a large number of Birmingham residents on the train.

Another fatal crash took place on 9 June, two days after the Rednal accident. This one turned out to be one of the best-remembered rail accidents of the nineteenth century due to one of its passengers, Charles Dickens. The accident happened at 2.30 pm and involved a train from Folkestone carrying passengers from the ferry from France. It occurred on a bridge at Staplehurst, where there had been some work taking place on the line. A plate had been left loose and the engine, on running over this, came off the line. The engine and part of the train stayed upright but the rest of the train, comprising seven or eight carriages, came off the bridge and fell down into the stream underneath.

When help arrived it was said that there was doubt as to whether some of the passengers died from the crushing of the carriages or from drowning in the stream. There were ten deaths. *The Times*'s report of 10 June mentioned

The railway accident at Staplehurst is particularly remembered for one of its surviving passengers, Charles Dickens. It was to have a great effect on the author's life.

that Dickens had had a narrow escape, which was fortunate for him as well as for literature. The unhurt passengers, including Dickens, had helped the injured.

Even though Dickens had sustained no injuries whatsoever in the Staplehurst crash it was to have a serious effect on him. Before the accident Dickens, who was interested in all aspects of society, was a regular rail traveller and was fascinated by how the new form of transport was changing people's lives.

Some of Dickens's fellow passengers died while he was trying to help them, including one man who was at first alive but was trapped and could not be released. Dickens lost his voice for two weeks following the accident. Medical opinion of the time was becoming increasingly aware of the emotional effects suffered by people involved in or witnessing an accident. Today we would probably call it post-traumatic stress. Dickens's son said that his father never recovered from the accident and afterwards avoided rail travel whenever possible.

The Staplehurst crash, as well as other distressing rail accidents of around that time, had an effect on Dickens's writing. One of his short stories, *The Signal-Man*, published in 1866, was a ghost story involving a train crash. In the postscript to *Our Mutual Friend*, Dickens's last published novel, he wrote of the Staplehurst crash: 'I remember with devout thankfulness that I can never be much nearer parting company with my readers for ever than I was then.' He had been carrying the transcript of the book when he was on board the fateful train.

The effect of the accident on Dickens's health was evident when he returned to America a few years afterwards. He was in poor health throughout the trip and still avoided rail travel if he possibly could. He did, however, make one eventful rail trip in 1868. On a train to Boston he met a 12-year-old girl called Kate Wiggin, who went on to become a kindergarten teacher and children's writer. She published her first book in 1883 but is most famous for *Rebecca of Sunnybrook Farm*, which she published in 1903. In 1912 Kate published a biographical memoir entitled *A Child's Journey with Dickens*, so perhaps her chance meeting with the famous writer was the catalyst that spurred her into becoming a writer herself.

Five years to the day after the Staplehurst crash, Dickens died.

It was claimed that the Staplehurst accident could have been worse had it not been for a new braking system that was being used in addition to the ones on the guards' vans. These brakes were known as Creamers and were an American invention patented in 1853. They were of particular value in arresting the progress of runaway passenger carriages, using a spring, pawl and rope system that was activated in an emergency. However, further advances in railway technology saw trains becoming heavier and faster and by the 1870s the Creamer Safety Brake system was superseded by power brakes.

In June 1866 the Court of Chancellery at Lincolns Inn heard the case of Roche versus the Midland Railway Company. The case was in regard to injuries concerning an accident that occurred on 15 August 1865 at Wellingborough. Mr Roche had been knocked unconscious, had been in bed for weeks after the accident and had not been able to work.

The Midland Railway Company did not contest negligence in regard to the accident. They were arguing over the extent of the man's injuries and the amount that he claimed to have normally earned when in employment. A doctor claimed Roche was suffering from Nervous Prostration and it would take up to two years for him to recover fully. Roche said that he normally earned between £600 and £700 per annum.

The railway company had obviously investigated Roche and claimed he had in fact been injured in a fight before the accident. They also claimed that he only earned £300 and had never paid any tax. The jury took Roche's side, as they normally did in these cases, and awarded him £850.

Although Charles Dickens may have been unhurt in the Staplehurst accident its influence on his attitude to rail travel later became apparent. On 29 January 1867 *The Times* published a letter from him in which he warned the public about a morning express train on the Midland Railway between Leicester and Bedford.

Dickens explained that he 'had never been so shaken and flung about as in this train.' At Market Harborough the passengers had complained to the railway officials. This also happened at Bedford. Dickens was told that the line was rough and he had been in a light carriage. Although he had a ticket to London, he and his travelling companion decided to leave the train at Bedford.

There was an interesting case in Edinburgh Court in April 1867 when the North British Railway Company claimed that they had no responsibility for an accident near Berwick-upon-Tweed in April 1866 in which Mr Athole James Hay had been injured. The accident was caused by a mail train hitting a truck that was loose on the line. The company claimed this was due to 'malicious mischief' from someone who had put the truck on the line.

There were no details of Mr Hay's injuries in the newspaper report of the case, only that he was a wine merchant from Leith. Lord Kinloch presiding told the jury that if they were satisfied the company were at fault for letting the truck get on the line then they were responsible for the man's injuries. The jury awarded him £500.

The *Cheshire Observer* published an article on 10 June stating that railway accidents rarely came singly and reminded the public of the danger of rail travel. As the excursion season started, so did the railway accident season.

A letter in *The Times* on 13 June 1865 concerned keys to railway carriage doors. It was signed 'A Railway Traveller in Daily Peril'. The writer quoted the Lord Advocate in a lecture in 1864 saying, 'Posterity will say, "Would you believe a hundred years ago they locked travellers in a box?"' A Mr Filder was quoted in the letter as saying, 'No man with a head on his shoulders knowing anything of railway travel would travel on the Brighton line without a door key.'

There was obviously some dispute over whether passengers should possess keys to carriage doors. Frederick North, a railway chairman, had strong opinions against the possession of railway carriage keys, believing it might endanger the lives of hundreds of people. In the Commons in June 1865 Sir W. Gallwey asked the president of the Board of Trade to prevent the future locking of railway doors, while Sir L. Palk asked if the locking of doors was legal.

A fatal accident occurred on 29 June 1867 on the London and North Western Railway; eight people died when a passenger train and a coal train collided at Warrington.

There seems to have been an attempt by newspapers at this time to publish more exclusive stories relating to railway accidents. *The Birmingham Daily Post* of 1 July called it 'an accident of the most deplorable character', and explained that the area where the accident occurred was not a passenger station but a semaphore station that had control over six to seven sets of points.

There was a terrible accident when three trains collided in the Welwyn Tunnel on the Great Northern Line in 1866. Two people were killed.

The passenger train was the 10.23 am from Liverpool to London via Birmingham. The train left Warrington Bank Quay Station at 11.25 and on approaching Walton Junction the driver saw a coal train ahead, which was being shunted onto the Chester line. He did not slow down because he expected the coal train to be clear by the time he reached it. Unfortunately, the points had not been altered and when the passenger train reached the junction it crashed into the coal train.

The driver and fireman of the passenger engine survived, having jumped clear. The first three carriages of the train were smashed to pieces. The worst affected was a Second Class carriage. Five of the passengers in this carriage died instantly. Another three were to die later from their injuries.

There was further mention of locked carriage doors in relation to this accident. A passenger in the carriage following the one most severely damaged saw the collision as it was about to occur and tried to jump off the train. He could not do this as the door had been locked.

The year 1868 was to see the most serious railway accident yet in Britain. There were thirty-three deaths on 20 August 1868 in an accident at Abergele on the Chester and Holyhead Railway.

The Birmingham Daily Post's headline stated: 'Irish mail on fire, twenty-three burned to death'. In the main body of its report it described the accident as 'the most extraordinary and fatal accident ever known on the English railway'. The information apparently came from an electric telegraph and the text was also reported word for word in *The Daily News* of the same day. Dublin's *The Freeman's Journal* published a different story but then included another version from an electric telegraph that was exactly the same as *The Birmingham Daily Post's* and *The Daily News's* reports.

It would seem then that in the event of an accident telegraphs were sent to a number of newspapers, which then resulted in similar stories being published. It was interesting that the *Dundee Courier & Argus* on the same day concentrated their story on how Lord and Lady Farnham had died in the accident while Lord Abercorn and his party had survived.

The accident involved the Irish Limited Mail train from London, which left at 7.15 am and passed Abergele Station about one o'clock. A goods train had passed half an hour before. At some point part of the goods train had become detached from the rest and had run back down an incline. The loose part of the goods train then met the Irish mail train, travelling at about 40 miles per hour. There was a curve just before the two trains met so the driver of the mail train, Arthur Thompson, saw the loose trucks just in time to be able to jump off the engine.

The last carriage of the loose goods train had contained petroleum oil. As the trains collided the petroleum ignited. The engine, tender and the first three carriages of the mail train were smashed to pieces and on fire. Eyewitness accounts said that for some time the whole of the line was covered in a sheet of flame. As the fire was being put out in one spot it would start again in another. The first three carriages were reduced to a few inches of ash on the ground. The only recognizable body was that of the fireman on the engine but it was a skeleton.

It was at first believed that the death toll was twenty-three but it was difficult to be certain due to the severe damage to the bodies. The final death toll was thirty-three. Identification of the bodies was only possible by items found on them such as jewellery and watches. A watch was found among the dead that had an inscription to Lord Farnham. It was at first believed he had been travelling with his two daughters.

There was no list of passengers for the train but persons missing included Jude Berwick, who had been seen talking to Lord Farnham at Chester. Later reports gave the names of some of the dead. It was not two of Lord Farnham's daughters amongst the dead but his wife and four servants. The Reverend Sir Nicholas and Lady Chinnery, and Captain and Mrs Townsend also died.

An accident at Beckenham in 1866 was another that was due to the collapse of a bridge. Engineering structures during the nineteenth century were often faulty.

The final fatal accident of the decade occurred on 9 October 1869 at Long Eaton, near Nottingham, on the Midland Railway. Once again it involved a special train for an outing. It was the time of the annual October fair at Nottingham.

The Daily News reported that a painful sensation was caused when one of the excursions that had gone to Nottingham had collided on its return journey. *The Leeds Mercury* explained that it was the last day of the Nottingham Goose Fair and the accident involved the last special from Nottingham.

A number of special trains were put on from the towns around Nottingham, three of them from Leicester. They had all arrived safely and the first two left for home in the evening. The last of the three Leicester specials left Nottingham at 11.40 pm. It was a very foggy evening and as the special train approached the Long Eaton Junction there was a luggage train on the line. There had been a problem with the couplings of the luggage train and it was held up, but there was no collision and the luggage train eventually moved off.

Meanwhile, the North Derby Mail train had left Nottingham only ten minutes after the special. There was an assumption that the special train had not been delayed as no one at Nottingham was aware of the problem with the luggage train. Then, due to the poor visibility caused by the fog, the mail train ran into the back of the special.

Although there were seven deaths on the special train there were very few injuries. In fact, those in the fifth carriage from the rear of the special were not even aware that there had been a collision. They were said to be laughing and singing and had no idea why the train had stopped. A number of the accidents that occurred around this time seem to have been due to the running of trains too closely together on the same line, which didn't allow for any hold-up to the train in front.

On the same day that many of the reports of the accident appeared in the newspapers there was a very detailed headline in the *Sheffield and Rotherham Independent* concerning another accident involving a group of men working on the line: 'Shocking decapitation on the Midland Railway near Rotherham'.

The accident occurred at a spot where ganger William Eason, aged sixty, was in charge of some plate-layers laying new rails. It was his duty to see that they worked properly and safely, but it seems that he did not apply his duties to taking care of his own safety.

The workers were given a timetable of the trains due on the lines they were working on. There was a down passenger train and an up goods train due at the same time. Instead of keeping to the 6-foot gap between the lines, Eason was standing on one of the tracks. As the goods train approached on the line he was standing on he heard it and moved off the track. Instead of staying in the space between the lines, however, he stepped onto the down track. It was on this line that the passenger train from Leeds was approaching.

According to evidence from Eason's landlady, he had been suffering from increasing deafness – not an ailment that someone responsible for hearing trains coming is happy to suffer with. He did not hear the second train and was knocked down.

Two men from the platelayers' gang reached the spot first. They were very shocked to find Eason's body on the track. His severed head was lying several feet away. They lifted both parts and placed them on a trolley. They then took Eason's remains to Masbro Station, where he was laid out in the stable at the Prince of Wales Hotel and was no doubt on view for whoever wanted to take a look.

CHAPTER 7

1870 to 1880

The beginning of a new decade did little to improve safety on the railways in Britain. In fact, as far as accidents were concerned, the year 1870 was to be one of the worst since rail travel had begun. There were no less than five fatal accidents during the year, ranging from five to fifteen fatalities each. There were three accidents in the month of December alone.

In a letter to *The Times* on 1 February 1870 a man claimed that, as a railway shareholder, he was a criminal. His punishment, he said, was disproportionate to the offences that he had on his conscience. The man was writing about the damages paid to those injured on the railways and the loss of his dividends due to the amounts paid out by railway companies. He argued that if all means were taken to ensure railways were run safely, then how could they be held responsible for accidents? He went on to argue that the owners of other forms of transport such as steam ships or omnibuses were not liable for damages in the case of accidents. This situation would become worse, he said, if they were forced to run workmen's trains that would be subsidized with cheap fares. While running at a loss, they would still be liable for damages from these passengers if they had an accident.

The Great Northern Railway began operating in 1846, despite opposition from the Midland Railway, who already ran services to York, which the GNR wanted to provide as well. Their safety record had been very good for quite some time but when there was another fatal accident, it was a serious one, with eighteen deaths on 20 June 1870.

According to *The Times*, the accident was 'one of most disastrous railway accidents that has ever happened'. It occurred between Newark and Claypole and involved a large excursion train with thirty carriages returning from a trip to London. As it passed a goods train at about 1.00 am it struck a wagon that had come off the line and turned over.

There were various numbers of fatalities given. *The Northern Echo* on 22 June gave the total number of dead as sixteen. They reported that the incident was on a day trip to London that gave twelve hours in the capital. *The Birmingham Daily Post* gave a more personal report about passenger William Pitts, who spent four hours trapped in a ditch. Bodies had dammed up the water, preventing it from filling the ditch but at one point the water was still deep enough to fill Pitts's mouth.

The train had also rolled into a ditch and most of the carriages were smashed to pieces. It was thought at first that fourteen were dead but then two more bodies were found. A number of people were injured, not all of whom were expected to survive.

The Times printed a statement by Mr Henry Oakley, Secretary of the GNR. He said that the wagon on the goods train was thrown onto the line in front of the excursion train when its axle had broken and that the goods wagon belonged to another railway line, but did not say which one. He claimed that the number of deaths was up to sixteen.

More details were revealed about the excursion train to London, which arrived at 8.30 that morning. It was made up of eight carriages from Leeds with 150 passengers, four carriages from Bradford with eighty-five passengers, five carriages from Halifax with eighty-three passengers and six carriages from York with seventy passengers. Four carriages were First Class and all the others were covered. The return fares to London were sixteen shillings First Class and eight shillings for the rest. Around eighty passengers also bought insurance tickets.

The inquiry into the accident was adjourned a number of times and did not conclude until 28 June. By this time the number of dead had risen to eighteen. There was some criticism by the coroner of an article that had appeared in *The Leeds Mercury* accusing some persons of plundering the dead. This was not an isolated claim and such instances were reported at other accidents.

The jury found that the deaths were due to the accidental breakage of an axle on the goods wagon belonging to the Manchester, Sheffield and Lincolnshire Railway. They went on to say that the goods train had been travelling too fast and the axle was not fit for use due to age. They recommended there should be an age limit set for the use of parts such as axles.

The Board of Trade Report was written by Captain H.W. Tyler. He recorded that a wheel had come off the leading axle of a carriage on the goods train. It was an old axle but no examination would, according to Tyler, have found the defect. There was a list of the carriages and their towns of origin. Tyler also mentioned that 381 tickets had been sold for the excursion but it wasn't known how many people were actually on the train at the time of the accident.

Another fatal accident occurred on the London and North Western Railway at Harrow on 26 November 1870. There were seven deaths and *The Times* called it an appalling accident. It involved the Liverpool Express, which left Euston at 5.00 pm.

The service had been running safely for many years but an increase in traffic on the L&NWR had led to the express being pulled by two engines until it reached Wolverton. It was a very large train, with a number of carriages bound for different locations. As it reached Harrow there was a problem. An empty coal train had left Willesden and was due to stop at Harrow to allow the express to pass. As the coal train was going into sidings some of the trucks broke free from the train and were left on the line. The express then hit the loose trucks.

Signals had been set but due to the fog they were not seen. There were seven deaths and a number of injuries. A passenger on the following train said that signals were burning brightly but that it was a very foggy evening. *The Birmingham Daily Post* of 28 June reported that the driver of one of the engines was nowhere to be found.

December 1870 was to see a chain of accidents. The first occurred on the North Eastern Railway on 6 December at Brockley Whins. *The Times* described it as the 'most frightful in the north for years'.

The accident involved the express from Newcastle to Sunderland, which left Sunderland at 10.30 am, and a coal train, of which there were a number in the area. The train contained a number of passengers heading for the markets in Newcastle.

The accident was due to a mistake by the pointsman, Hedley, who was arrested. Brockley Whins Station had one platform, which was served by up and down traffic. The express was approaching the station from the east but was not due to stop there. A coal train for Tyne Dock was coming from the west. As the two trains approached, Hedley got mixed up, and instead of opening the points to the dock for the coal train, he opened the points for the station. This also opened the points from the main line, sending both trains onto the same line at the platform.

The carriage following the engine was so badly damaged that passengers were thrown onto the two crashed engines. One of the dead was Mr Frederick Younge, a well-known local actor. Also on the train were other members of the cast of the play in which the deceased had been playing; they were injured but survived. A man named Taplin, who was a porter but had been put on

In 1876 there was a collision between an express and a coal train in a blizzard at Abbots Ripton. Coal was one of the main loads for goods trains in the nineteenth century.

the train as a temporary guard, was reported to have had the bones in his legs crushed to powder. There were five fatalities and a very large number of injured, totalling fifty-seven. As the accident occurred in a major coal mining area it was no surprise that the *Evening Gazette* reported that a local coal owner, Mr W.B. Ogden, was taken out of the wreckage alive but died half an hour later.

The worst accident of the month took place on 12 December, on the Manchester, Sheffield and Lincolnshire Railway at Stairfoot. The accident was due to what seemed to have been a common cause in recent years. While a goods train was being shunted at Barnsley a number of the trucks became detached and ran back down the line. At Stairfoot, 2 miles from Barnsley, the trucks met the 6.05 pm passenger train from Barnsley to Sheffield. The train was standing at the station platform. The brake van and two of the carriages were smashed to pieces.

The first report in *The Times* gave the numbers as fourteen dead and twenty injured, the same numbers given by *The Birmingham Daily Post*. The actual numbers were fifteen dead and fifty-nine injured.

It was some time before help arrived from Barnsley on special trains. This included many of the local surgeons. According to the *Evening Gazette* the delay in getting help was due to the fact that there was no telegraph line between Stairfoot and Barnsley.

There had been some local help from miners who were nearby celebrating the Oak's Colliery Anniversary. There was a strange connection between disasters here. The anniversary was of an explosion at the colliery four years earlier, in 1866, in which 380 people died. Both disasters occurred on the date of 12 December.

Although they had few accidents, those that did occur on the Great Northern Railway seemed spectacular. A fatal accident occurred on the line on 26 December 1870, the third fatal accident of that month. The eight deaths included passengers as well as some bystanders.

Due to the timing of the accident details were slow in being reported. The *Dundee Courier & Argus* had a brief paragraph relating to the accident but said that details were not available due to the celebration of Christmas. On the same day, however, 27 December, *The Standard* published a letter from Mr H. Oakley, the manager of the GNR, giving details of the accident, with the number of dead as seven passengers and a signalman's wife.

The train was a fast one from King's Cross to Peterborough, which was due to stop at Hatfield. It had a brake van next to the engine, a Second and a First Class carriage and then five other carriages, followed by a guard's van. It reached a point called Bell's Bar, midway between Potter's Bar and Hatfield stations, where there was a gated level crossing. There was also a gatekeeper's cottage on the down side line.

The gatekeeper, Henry Long, was standing on the up line as the train arrived. As it passed the crossing the brake van behind the engine broke away. The First and Second Class carriages were smashed to pieces. Parts of the train struck the gatekeeper's cottage. The gate on the up side was also damaged. There were about thirty to forty passengers who were unhurt and they helped those who had been less fortunate.

The Times's report noted that there was an unusual result of the accident in that the dead outnumbered the injured, which is very uncommon in railway accidents. There were at the time seven bodies found and five injured, who were taken to the local cottages. There was heavy snow falling at the time of the accident.

Another of the injured, a Mr Potter, was treated by a doctor but died about thirty minutes after the accident occurred. The passengers who died were all from the Second Class carriage but only six of the eight fatalities were passengers. The others were part of a group who had been walking on the line.

There were four people walking to the signal box. They were Mrs Oswin, the signalman's wife, her sister-in-law, named Kershaw, a young man and a youth. The two women had been killed but the two men were only injured. The bodies were not all identified at the time.

Identification of the bodies was not always an exact science. One of the male victims was found to have more than £100 in his pocket. For some reason he was identified as a Mr Wren, a fishmonger from Luton. Anyone who had heard of his death in the accident must have been shocked to see him alive and well walking around in Hatfield. The dead man was in fact Mr Branston, a cattle dealer from Stilton.

The enquiry into the accident took place a few days later. Unusually it was not held in a public house but in a school, in Welham. The coroner was Mr Grove Lowe of St Albans. Present were a number of employees of the Great Northern Railway, including Mr Meadows White.

The accident had been caused by what seems to be one of the more common reasons for fatalities on the railway – a broken tyre. When the tyre broke the axle was damaged, which also led to the brake van coming free from the engine. The representatives of the company claimed that all the wheels of the train were inspected and tested before being used. The fact that this seemed to make little difference in relation to accidents when such defects in the wheels occurred never seemed to be mentioned.

The coroner summed up by saying that the accident occurred due to the breaking of a tyre due to the friction of the metal when the weather was very cold. Metal was subject to this failure and this was a danger against which it was thought impossible to guard.

The opinion of the coroner appears to show that there was an acceptance of the chances of such an accident occurring on any journey undertaken by a train. Although this accident may have occurred in cold weather there were other examples of tyres breaking in warmer weather, so it seems that people travelled on the railways at their own risk knowing the chance of an accident was quite high.

After the terrible month of December 1870 there was to be some relief for railway travellers; the next fatal accident did not occur for almost two years. This time it was on the Caledonian Railway at Kirtlebridge Station, 17 miles north of Carlisle.

There were a number of sidings at the station and on the day of the accident a mineral train from Carlisle arrived there at 7.55 am. This was unusual in that the train normally arrived there thirty-five minutes after the night express from London arrived at the station. On this day, however, the express was almost two hours late, after being held up at Greyrigg.

The mineral train left some trucks at the station and was then supposed to go onto the up line while the express passed. For some reason the pointsman sent the train onto the down line. The signals for the express were at this point all set for clear so it continued at full speed.

The express was a heavy train with eighteen carriages and two engines. As there was a curve just before the station the driver could not see the mineral train until the last minute. One eyewitness said the train hit the mineral wagon so hard that some of the trucks were thrown up in the air and landed some distance away. The express carried on pushing some wagons in front of it until they hit part of the station. The station clock stopped at 8.13 am when the train hit the building.

Another witness statement in *The Daily News* said that among the eleven dead were three women and a girl. His version was that, apart from the two wagons that flew through the air, two more stayed on the line before the train eventually crashed into the booking office at the station.

The accident illustrates that the random chances of being safe or in danger was dependent on where on the train you were sitting. The first carriage was undamaged, as were those at the end of the train. It was the second, third and fourth carriages that were destroyed. It was from these carriages that the majority of the dead came. The engine driver of the first engine was also a fatality. There were twelve deaths and many injured.

There were a number of coincidences involving railway workers where members of the same family were killed while working on the lines. There was an interesting incident of this kind reported in the *Illustrated Police News* in November 1872. It involved a female navvy, Caroline Metcalfe, who was killed by an express train near Bradford. Her husband had been killed on the same line twenty years earlier, since which time she had been working on the railways and said that she would work at no other labour. It was not the coincidence that led to the report but the fact that she was a female navvy breaking stones for twelve shillings a week.

The next fatal accident took place at Wigan on 2 August 1873. It was on the London and North Western Railway. The accident was quite unusual in that it was not due to a collision but still led to thirteen deaths and thirty being injured.

The train involved was the express from London to Scotland. According to *The Birmingham Daily Post* it was a Scottish tourist express and was one of the heaviest trains of the season. It left Euston just after 8.00 pm, about five minutes late. It was a large train with twenty-two carriages, three vans and two engines. It was fifteen minutes late when it passed Wigan Station at 1.18 am.

The train had almost passed through the station at 40 miles an hour when for some reason the last seven or eight carriages broke free and went into a siding while the train carried on along the main line. The carriages that had broken free smashed into the station platform and a number of them came off the wheels and turned over onto the platform.

Much of the station building was damaged, along with a wall alongside the station. Part of a carriage and the body of a woman were thrown onto the roof of a nearby foundry. There were a number of workers in the foundry on a night shift but none of them were injured.

There were twelve deaths – again it was chance as to who received the fatal injuries. One family travelling in the same compartment lost two children while another survived. The mother was seriously injured but the father escaped unhurt. Two women survived the crash and then died as they were taken to the waiting room.

The results of a railway accident at Wigan in 1878. Accidents often occurred at a station, which made it easier to get help for the victims.

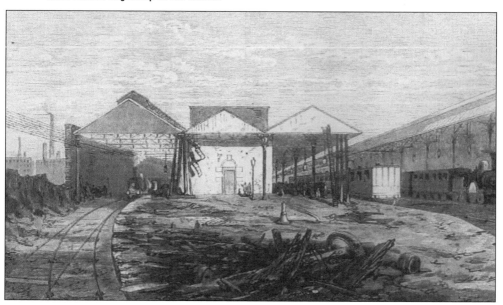

The Daily News gave the melancholy news of the death of Sir John Anderson. The details were given to his wife in town and she was to travel to the scene to be with her daughters, who had also been involved in the accident. One can't help gaining the impression that the death of someone from the upper classes was seen as more important than a passenger from a Third Class compartment.

An accident occurred on 2 December 1873 between two goods trains on the Cornwall Railway at Menheniot. The railway there was single line working and the accident occurred because of a misunderstanding by a guard.

There were two trains waiting to use the single line, one up and one down. The man on duty at Menheniot Station went to change the points for the down train and called out 'all right'. The guard on the up train thought the words were addressed to him and moved off. The two trains met on the single line. Three drivers and three stokers were hurt (one of the trains had two engines), and one of the drivers later died.

The Daily Gazette reported how the guard of the train that was struck from the rear jumped off at the moment of impact as his van was smashed to pieces. There was great difficulty digging the injured out of the wreckage.

A serious accident occurred on the Glasgow to Edinburgh line of the North British Railway on 27 January 1874. The accident, due to a collision between a passenger train and a mineral train, resulted in sixteen deaths and numerous injuries. *The Bradford Observer* reported that there was great consternation on the Glasgow Royal Exchange at the news of the accident.

There was probably more consternation at the site of the accident as it was reported that bodies were lying in large numbers at the side of the line. Many had been cut to pieces. *The Daily News* reported that all the passengers in one Third Class carriage were killed. One of the dead was unknown but they published the address of a letter found in the lady's pocket.

The passenger train was an early morning one from Edinburgh. As it travelled along the main line a mineral train came onto the up line from the Monkland system. They collided at Bo'ness Junction below a stone bridge. Half the bridge was destroyed in the collision.

The driver of the passenger train died instantly. The first carriage was a Third Class one and was broken to pieces. All the passengers in this carriage were killed. There were also some deaths in the following Second Class carriage. Two horses in a horsebox were also killed.

The Times stated that the danger signals were set against the passenger train. The morning was clear so there were no visibility problems. The accident occurred at 7.23 am. It seems that the driver did not take any notice of the signals.

There was to be one of the most serious accidents to occur on British railways in September 1874. There were twenty-five deaths after a collision on 10 September near Norwich on the Great Eastern Railway. Even before the total number of deaths was known, the *Essex County Standard* was stating that it was one of the most fearful in the district. They were reporting the fatalities then as fifteen or sixteen.

A mail train had left Yarmouth at 8.40 pm and was joined at Reedham by a train from Lowestoft. The train reached Brundall and after this point the line was single working, so the train had to wait so that the express from Norwich to Yarmouth could pass.

The train was then allowed to proceed onto the single line. Then the express was allowed to leave Norwich at the same time. The collision took place at Thorpe, which is about 2 miles from Norwich. There was a curve in the line so neither driver saw the other until just before they met at about 50 miles per hour.

The drivers and firemen of both trains died instantly. Luckily there was a doctor and a surgeon on the mail train. However, the surgeon was so badly injured he could not help. As well as the twenty-five deaths there were more than seventy passengers injured. The *Essex County Standard* reported that the two engines reared up into a perpendicular position.

There were some advantages as to where the collision took place. The Norwich train had just crossed the bridge over the river Yare. If the collision had occurred there many more could have died from falling into the river. For some reason there were three empty carriages behind the engine of the Norwich train.

The Birmingham Daily Post was more concerned with the bodies of the dead. They mentioned that the bodies were placed on hastily erected beds in a village inn. One man lay next to a 5-year-old child. A woman was so badly crushed that she looked like a chaotic mass of clothing. Reporters were evidently allowed to view the bodies. I have read of other disasters where bodies were brought out into the open so they could be photographed.

The most serious railway accident to occur so far in Britain, at least in regard to the number of fatalities, took place on Christmas Eve 1874 on the GWR, when thirty-four people died. There is never a good time for a rail accident but for such a horrific event to occur on Christmas Eve makes it seem even worse. *The Daily News* no doubt wanted to emphasize the point by saying that the train was heavily laden with passengers en route to visit relatives.

The accident at Shipton on Cherwell, Christmas Eve 1874. This was a time of year when the trains were usually very crowded.

The disaster took place near Shipton-on-Cherwell, close to Oxford. The train, from Oxford to Birmingham, was quite full and had thirteen carriages and two engines. The tyre of a wheel on a Third Class carriage broke about 6 miles into the journey. The train then passed over the bridge across the Cherwell but before crossing another bridge over the Oxford and Birmingham Canal the carriage fell down an embankment. *The Liverpool Mercury* of Christmas Day spread the season's cheer with the headline: 'Train leaves line and plunges into canal, terrible scenes'.

The train had been travelling at 40 miles an hour and the force of the carriage that had broken free took others with it. One carriage then fell into the canal. According to the report in *The Times*, bodies were strewn everywhere and heart-rending shrieks emanated from the injured.

Those passengers who were not injured were aided by workers from the nearby Hampton Gay paper mill. According to the manager of the mill, Mr Pearson, it was at least an hour before any help came from nearby railway stations and at least another half an hour before a doctor arrived. One passenger from a carriage that was undamaged went down the line with a red rug to signal any approaching trains to stop.

Many of the injured were taken to the Radcliffe Infirmary in Oxford. Others went to the Manor House in Hampton Gay. Those who arrived in Oxford went to the New College, Joni's Railway Hotel, the Randolph Hotel and the King's Arms Hotel. The report went on to list the names of those at the infirmary.

Stories about the accident continued to be published in *The Times* for some time afterwards. As well as information on the resulting enquiries there were also some personal stories, such as one from a Mrs Mitchell from the Boat Inn at Thrupp who had taken in a young girl of three who had been injured in the accident. She suspected that the girl's parents had died and requested *The Times* to publish details and a description of the girl to locate any family.

There was also a statement published from a man named John Mullee. He

A view of the interior of a carriage after the Shipton-on-Cherwell crash. The fact that the carriage had sides and a roof point to it being First Class.

claimed to have been a passenger in the Third Class carriage on which the wheel had broken leading to the accident. He claimed that the carriage had been in for repair at Oxford Station but that due to a lack of another Third Class carriage, it had still been fixed to the train.

As well as the inquests into the deaths there was a Board of Trade enquiry into the accident. It was written by Colonel W. Yolland, who explained that the train was made up of a mixture of four- and six-wheeled trucks. The train had a Harrison cord communication system fitted from the guard's van to a bell or gong on the tender.

There was some dispute explained in the report. A representative of the GWR had said that up to the end of 1871, inquiries into accidents and collisions were unauthorized by any Act of Parliament. They had been directed by the Board of Trade and the commissioners of railways and could make suggestions but had no power. Since 1871, however, they were authorized under the Regulations of the Railways Act. One of the early problems that had been found was a lack of braking power on passenger trains.

The accident that occurred on 28 August 1875 was, although serious, much lighter in the number of fatalities than the ones that it followed. This accident occurred on the Midland Railway at Kildwick, near Skipton, and resulted in five deaths. It was the result of a collision between two passenger trains.

The end of the month wasn't a good time for the railways. *The Daily Gazette* reported the accident at Kildwick and also went on to report on a less serious accident in the Ambergate Tunnel on the London to Scotland line and on a goods train that was derailed at Chesterfield.

The Kildwick accident occurred on a Saturday evening at 11.25. The Scottish express to Leeds ran into an excursion train at Kildwick. The excursion train had left Bradford and was returning to Morecambe. As it approached Kildwick Station the danger signal was against it so it slowed down. The Scottish express then crashed into the back of it.

It is thought that the excursion train should have passed through the station and the danger signal should then have stopped the express before the station. The dead and most of the injured were on the final carriages of the excursion train.

Excursion trains still seemed to have been a dangerous form of travel. In September 1875 the increase in trips from London to Southend led to a fatal accident. Five excursion trains were travelling back from the coast in quick succession. Two collided near Barking, leading to one death and many injuries.

A train caught in a flood near Newark in 1875. It seems as if the train has been washed off the line.

The enquiry blamed the driver of the second train in the collision for recklessness but there was also criticism for making up such large excursion trains. The London, Tilbury and Southend Railway paid out £20,000 to the injured.

Despite its early good safety record, the Great Northern Railway was having a bad decade in the 1870s. The third fatal accident of the decade involving the company took place in January 1876. It happened at Abbots Ripton Station, just north of Huntingdon. There was heavy snow falling at the time. The first report in *The Times* was published on 22 January. *The Daily News* of the same day reported that a telegram had been received at the GNR offices at King's Cross, with brief details of the accident.

A coal train consisting of around thirty trucks arrived at the station and was signalled to go into a siding to allow the express from Edinburgh to King's Cross to pass. Before all the trucks had passed into the siding the express arrived at full speed as it was not due to stop there. The engine hit the last three or four trucks at high speed and turned over on its side. Several of the carriages were completely smashed to pieces. Then the express from King's

Cross to Edinburgh came in the opposite direction and hit the debris. Amazingly, it was at first reported that only three passengers were killed and a large number injured. A number of officers of the company were travelling on the up express. One of these, Mr Cleghorn, suffered a broken arm.

Two days later, on 24 January, *The Times* went into more detail. It seems that the coal train was eighteen minutes late. This led to the first collision. After this occurred the signals were set to red to warn the express from King's Cross. Fog signals were also set to warn the driver but due to the heavy snowfall he did not see the signals or hear the fog warnings and crashed into the wreckage from the first collision.

It was not until the report of 24 January that it was confirmed that in fact there had been eighteen deaths, not three, as first reported. One of these, a Mr Jolliffe from the Isle of Wight, was a passenger on the first express to London. After the accident he went to help others, having not been injured himself. While inspecting the turned-over engine of his own train, the express from London arrived without Mr Jolliffe seeing it. The engine of the train hit the wreckage and turned over, crushing him.

When the number of deaths became known the *Lancaster Gazette* called it the most disastrous accident in connection with the railways for some time. The regularity of fatal accidents must have been acceptable as it had been only just over a year since thirty-four people had died in an accident.

There was obviously some concern at the circumstances of the accident and Sir Charles Adderley, president of the Board of Trade, called on Mr Forbes, the secretary of the Great Northern Railway Company at King's Cross. It is believed that Captain Tyler, the inspector of the Railway Department of the Board of Trade, would inquire into the circumstances of the accident.

The headlines relating to railway crashes had been toned down by this time. When fifteen people died on the Somerset and Dorset Railway on 7 August 1876, the headline in *The Times* stated a reserved, 'Railway Accident'. However, the report did take a more outspoken line, beginning by calling it a 'fearful accident'. *The Birmingham Daily Post* said that it was the worst ever in the district. The line had only been open two years.

The accident took place at Radstock. It was a head-on collision on single track working. The line was worked by the Somerset and Dorset Railway and connected the Midland, and the London and South Western railways.

An excursion train from Bournemouth to Bath stopped at a siding just after Radstock, where there was a colliery siding. As it began to move again a train from Bath to Radstock came from the opposite direction on the single line and collided with the excursion train. The fifteen deaths and most of the injuries occurred on the train to Radstock.

There was some dispute about what had happened. The signalman at Foxcote Siding said that he had no notice of the approach of the Radstock train. Other officials contradicted him and a policeman said that half an hour after the collision he saw the signal lights were out. It was later reported that this was due to a lack of oil.

The Board of Trade appointed Captain Tyler, assisted by barrister Mr W. Ravenhill, to hold a public inquiry into the causes of the accident. This was held at Bath.

The decade continued to be a bad one for the Great Northern. Less than a year after the disaster at Abbots Ripton, another fatal accident occurred on the same line near Hitchin, at the Arlesey Siding Station. The first report in *The Times* on Christmas Day 1876 gave the number of deaths as five, with thirty injured.

Once again it seemed that the accident was due to a goods train being shunted onto a siding and not clearing the main line quickly enough. This time it was a luggage train and two of the trucks came off the tracks, stopping it getting into the sidings before the express came up and hit it. Six carriages were completely destroyed.

The bodies of the driver and fireman of the express were found 100 yards before the crash site. It is thought that they both jumped out of the engine before the collision occurred. The dead were moved to the Lamb Inn by the station. The injured went to a nearby asylum, whose medical staff had come to help.

It was later reported that, rather than moving the goods train to allow the express to pass, it was directed onto the siding to pick up more trucks by a signalman, who then set the signal to danger. The wheels of one of the trucks became jammed in the line, causing two other trucks to come off the rails.

The inquiry took place on Christmas Day at Arlesey Siding Station. It was overseen by Captain Tyler, the government inspector, and was attended by a number of officials of the Great Northern Railway.

The guard from the express said that he was sorting parcels as they approached the station and not looking for signals. It was when he heard the driver whistle that he applied his brakes. He looked out and saw the signals were at red so he then held onto the brake wheel as the collision occurred.

The enquiry was adjourned, to be renewed the following day at King's Cross. The problem facing the inquiry was why the driver had not stopped at the danger signal. In *The Times* on 28 December it was reported that this could have been due to the foggy atmosphere or perhaps the fact that the driver was colour blind and couldn't tell red from green – a dangerous affliction for a train driver if true.

There were an incredible number of cases of decapitation on railway lines, often involving people who were not actually train passengers. One of these incidents was reported in the *Lancaster Gazette* on 24 April 1878. A middle-aged lady, Mrs Drewe, had been standing on a platform at Silverton Station in Devon. She was waiting for the arrival of a train carrying her husband, the proprietor of a paper mill. As a train approached the down line platform she rushed to meet it, attempting to cross the track in front of the engine. Unfortunately, it was not a train that stopped at the station and it hit her, severing her head from her body.

There was another collision on 19 October 1878 at Pontypridd, which resulted in thirteen deaths. It was on the Taff Vale Railway and took place at a junction for the Rhondda Valley branch of the railway. The *Lloyd's Weekly Newspaper* explained that it was due to an empty passenger train backing into a full passenger train. Ten died in a Third Class carriage, one of them being decapitated.

The normal operation was that the empty Llantrissant train would pull onto the north junction loop until the Rhondda train had passed into the

The Tay Bridge before the disaster. It was the longest railway bridge in the world when it opened in 1878. It was thought at the time that it was a miracle of engineering.

Old Tay Bridge from North (before disaster)

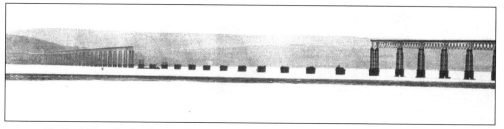

The Tay Bridge after the disaster. The area that collapsed can be seen where the train plunged into the river.

station. On the day of the accident there was an error; it seems that the drivers of both trains had the signals in their favour. The Llantrissant train was shunting backwards and ran into the Rhondda train. There was as a result a total of thirteen deaths and a number of injured. The *Aberdeen Weekly Journal* said that the cries of the injured were heard at the station 300 yards away.

The end of the year of 1879 was to see the worst accident by far to occur on British railways. On 28 December an estimated seventy-five people died when the Tay Bridge collapsed while a train was crossing it. The train belonged to the North British Railway.

There was once again some delay in the news becoming widely known due to the time of the year. Some newspapers were concentrating on the much less serious accident that had occurred at the Menai Bridge, where there had been no deaths. The *Dundee Courier* published a long article praising the construction of the Forth Railway Bridge on 30 December, which would seem inappropriate if they already knew about the Tay Bridge disaster.

When the news did become known the number of dead was overestimated, with the *Western Mail* claiming that 200 had died when a Scottish passenger train was blown into a river. *The Birmingham Daily Post* also reported: 'Tay Bridge Destroyed – 200 dead'. These reports were both published on 29 December.

The number of reported dead did decline slightly by the following day, 30 December, when the *York Herald* claimed, 'A great sensation has been caused in London by the awful railway disaster, the likes of which has not occurred in the memory of the oldest residents. Upwards of 100 lives lost.'

The accident occurred while a gale was blowing over Dundee and a train from Edinburgh was crossing the bridge when it collapsed. *The Times's* report of 29 December stated that the train was in the water under the bridge. Due to the gale, however, steamboats had not been able to reach the bridge to attempt rescue.

The train had entered the bridge from the Fife side at 7.14 pm going to Dundee. It was running along the rails when a flash of fire was seen. There was an attempt to reach the signal box at the north end of the bridge by the stationmaster from Dundee but the wires were broken. When the stationmaster went to look at the bridge he saw a large gap. At this point, however, he believed that the train had stopped before the break.

It was believed there were about 75 passengers on the train. The bridge stood nearly 90 feet above the river and the river itself was about 40 to 50 feet deep. The bridge was 2 miles long and was the longest in the world over a river at that time.

There was obviously some dispute over why the bridge had collapsed. Much of the blame was eventually placed on the man who designed and built the bridge, Sir Thomas Bouch. Part of the blame should have been placed on the North British Railway as well.

To save money they only wanted a single track bridge, which made it less stable. They also wanted a large enough space under the bridge for ships to pass beneath it. Bouch had asked lieutenant Colonel William Yolland RE for advice on the structure of the bridge. Yolland was then one of the men who took part in the enquiry. Yolland later became chief railway inspector.

The design was faulty in that lugs that held tie bars in place were made of cast iron, which was not suitable. The man responsible for maintenance on the bridge, Mr Noble, should also have shouldered some of the blame. He had no experience of such a task. When there was noise of rattling of parts of the bridge he stuck metal strips in the gaps, which stopped the noise but did nothing to stop the problem.

If the disaster at the Tay Bridge did anything, it made those responsible for constructing such large engineering tasks more careful with safety. Cast iron became used less as the properties of steel became better known.

CHAPTER 8

1880 to 1890

The decade began in normal fashion, although it was August before a serious fatal accident occurred. It was on the Midland Railway. Once again, the accident happened on a single stretch of line, and resulted in eight deaths.

It involved a small train of only eight carriages, which left Leeds at just after midday for Lancaster. *The Birmingham Daily Post* reported that the train consisted of only First and Third Class carriages. It had just passed Wennington Junction, where on this stretch of line there was only a single track – except at stations, where it was double, for shunting. There was no collision but the engine came off the track as it hit a set of points.

The train carried on off the line until it came to a bridge that crossed the track. The carriage behind the engine struck the bridge. It was smashed to pieces and the second carriage telescoped into it. The injured were taken to Lancaster Infirmary.

One of the passengers said he had been looking out of the carriage window when the train gave a jolt. It then kept jolting along until it got to the bridge.

The passenger jumped out as soon as the carriage struck the bridge. Two of his fellow passengers in the same compartment were amongst the dead. There were reports of crowds of people besieging Lancaster and Morecambe stations waiting for news of friends and relatives who were expected to be on the train.

It was almost a year before the next serious fatal accident occurred. This time it was on the Lancashire and Yorkshire Railway, near Blackburn. There was a collision between the Manchester Express and a train that was standing at Blackburn Station. There were seven deaths. *The Times* said there were a number of narrow escapes. One of these was a Mr Evans of the *Manchester Evening News*, who jumped off the train with his daughter a moment before the collision.

The driver of the express, Mr Standfield, said that all the signals were off

Another fallen bridge and crashed train on the Midland line near Hereford, in 1880.

as he approached the station. He also said that the Westinghouse brakes on the train did not work as they should have done and he did as much as he could to stop the train before the collision. Passengers on the train said that the carriages began to jump as the brakes were applied.

The Accrington correspondent of *The Times* said that the accident was the subject of much criticism. He said that it was considered a blunder to allow an express to approach within 20 to 30 yards of a station before applying the brake. The report didn't make it clear if the express was supposed to stop at the station or whether he meant that it should slow down and brake even if it wasn't supposed to stop.

March 1881 saw a case that showed the railway companies had become liable to pay damages in any situation where someone was hurt on the railway, despite their own negligence. The case was heard at Westminster Court and involved a Mr Wilkes and the North Eastern Railway Company.

The report did not mention where the accident happened but it seems that Mr Wilkes went through a small gate by a station and crossed the line. There was a clear sight of the line for up to 900 yards and it was broad daylight. However, Mr Wilkes did not look along the line before crossing and was hit by a train, which cut off his arm.

Despite his own carelessness Mr Wilkes was awarded £400. This was because the gate had been left open and the train had not whistled as it approached the station.

The new decade had seen an improvement in the number of accidents, with only one serious accident a year so far. The accident, in 1882, occurred on 27 November at Inverythan on the Great North of Scotland Railway, on the Macduff and Turriff branch line. There were five deaths. When *The Bristol Mercury* reported on the accident on 28 November they said that official accounts gave the number of deaths as five, but rumour stated fourteen.

The accident happened between Auchterless and Fyvie stations. It involved a mixed train of both passenger carriages and goods wagons. It was the practice of the railway to run such trains. The train left Macduff at 4.20 pm going to Aberdeen. The *Huddersfield Daily Chronicle* said it was an accident the likes of which had never occurred on the line before.

After leaving Auchterless the train reached a bridge over the Turriff Road, which was about 18 feet above the road. The engine and the guard's van passed safely over the bridge but when the three goods wagons following tried to pass over, the bridge collapsed. The goods wagons and the following passenger carriages fell down onto the road. One Third Class carriage teetered on the edge for a time before following the others down onto the road. There were two Third Class carriages as well as the goods trucks that fell. The only First Class carriage stayed on the line. The accident had happened in a very rural area so, apart from the surviving passengers, there was no one to help the injured. It was 8.15 before a relief train arrived.

The report went on to say that the bridge had been in a 'shaky state for some time'. It was under repair at the time of the accident and trains were supposed to slow down as they crossed it. The train was doing this but railway

The 1882 accident at Inverythan occurred when part of a train fell from yet another collapsed bridge.

An accident in a tunnel at Canonbury in 1881. Accidents in tunnels were even more frightening for passengers than those that happened in the open.

officials claimed that if it had been going at normal speed it would have crossed the bridge before it collapsed.

The Board of Trade report was written by Major F.A. Marindin. The major mentioned that the timber of the bridge had been renewed in 1871. The weakness had been in the cast iron girder on the east side of the bridge, which had broken in two. One end was still on the abutment while the other was on the ground. Marindin said that the weakness may have been spotted in the yard before the girder was painted but not once it was part of the bridge.

The early accidents of the 1880s seem to have been over-represented in Scotland. For the second year running, the worst accident on the railways was above the border. This time it was at Lockerbie Station, on 14 May 1883. The main line at the station was joined by a branch line from Stranraer at the north end of the station. At 11.30 pm a goods train was leaving the station on the main line heading north. It was passing the junction with the Stranraer line when an express from Stranraer hit the goods train. The *North-Eastern Daily*

Gazette had a specially telegraphed report on the accident. It said that the train was more than usually crowded with returning holidaymakers.

It is believed that the signals were against the express. The collision knocked some of the goods trucks onto the up line. Then the express from Glasgow that did not stop at Lockerbie ran into the upset trucks. The train was being pulled by two engines and was travelling at about 50 miles per hour. The first engine left the rails and hit the wooden platform, which collapsed. The train then hit another part of the platform, which was made of stone. The driver and firemen were killed instantly.

The tilted goods trucks tore the sides of most of the carriages on the express as the second engine continued to pull them along the line. One of the goods wagons was then thrown up onto the opposite platform. There were another five deaths, all of whom were passengers, including one baby.

There was a personal account of two men who had Third Class tickets but as the carriage was crowded they had been allowed to go into a sleeping saloon. They moved back to Third Class after some passengers got off. There were six passengers in the compartment. They had been sitting with their feet up on the opposite seats. As they heard the crash someone said to jump up onto the seats. They did this in case the seats were crushed together, trapping their legs. Despite this being one of the worst damaged carriages, all six of the passengers in this compartment got out unhurt.

The driver of the Stranraer train continued to argue that the signals gave him the right of way. The signalman and the stationmaster, however, claimed that they were at danger.

It would have been too much to expect the number of fatal accidents to stay at one a year and 1884 was to break the pattern. On 3 June there was an accident on the London and South Western Railway. It occurred on the Salisbury and Wimborne branch line. The train involved was the 4.30 pm from Salisbury. The train was very busy, it being market day in the town. *The Birmingham Daily Post* of 4 June had a report based on a telegram they received at midnight. The headline of the report was: 'Fall of train into river'.

The train reached the next station from Salisbury, which was Downton, but not the next, Bearmore. While travelling across a bridge over the river Avon the whole train left the rails as it went round a bend at 40 miles per hour. The engine stayed on the line but after about 100 yards the train fell down the embankment. One of the carriages was lying in a stream. The others were mainly destroyed.

The site of the accident was opposite the Downton College of Agriculture and the students quickly came out to help. There were, surprisingly, only four killed but more than forty were injured. A later account claimed that there were two engines pulling the train. It stated that the axle on the second engine broke and this caused the train to go down the embankment.

The second serious accident of the year took place little less than a month later, on the Manchester, Sheffield and Lincolnshire Railway. It was to be the first of a series of accidents that hit the railway. This one was on 16 July 1884 at Penistone and was one of the most serious for some time.

The train involved was the Manchester to King's Cross express, which left Manchester just after midday. The train had seven composite carriages, a horsebox and two brake vans. The driver, Sam Cawood, had been driving the train known as the 'newspaper train' for a number of years and so was very experienced.

The train reached Bullhouse Colliery, where the line ran across a bridge over Thurlstone Road, which is 2 miles from Penistone. As it passed the bridge the axle broke on the engine and almost the entire train came off the rails and fell down the embankment. The engine, tender and the horsebox stayed on the rails. The train had been travelling at 55 miles per hour and was very crowded.

A number of men from the colliery came to help but found that many of the carriages had been smashed to pieces. There were twenty-four dead and more than sixty injured. Those who had come off best seemed to have been in the centre of the train. The dead included three children. *The Times's* report stated that one seemed to have died while asleep but the other two had terror-stricken expressions and must have had warning of their deaths.

It was interesting that the report thought it was important to mention that one of the women found dead in a First Class carriage had £11 in her pocket. It did not mention her injuries but went into detailed descriptions of a number of the Third Class fatalities.

There was no doubt as to the cause of the accident. The broken crank axle was still visible. There was a drawing hook that connected the horsebox and the carriages. This had also broken, allowing the carriages to become detached from the rest of the train. It had broken as the train was going round the sharpest part of a curve.

One man gave a statement as to what had happened to him. He became trapped by the legs between two seats. His leg was broken and he could see the following carriage hanging over the bridge and looking as though it was about to fall on him. He saw some of the passengers in the overhanging carriage then fall out of it onto the road. The man was eventually released by railway workers.

There was an interesting mention of locked carriage doors by a passenger in the *Aberdeen Weekly Journal* of 17 July. He said that after feeling the carriage shaking, it rolled down an embankment the height of four carriages. He had a railway key, which he gave to those above him, who opened the carriage door so that they could escape.

The next serious fatal accident not only involved the same company as the last one, the Manchester, Sheffield and Lincolnshire Railway, it was just a few miles from Penistone, where the last accident had happened. It occurred on 1 January 1885 at 8.20 am. The *North-Eastern Daily Gazette* ran the headline: 'New Year opens with a terrible railway accident'. The accident happened between the Barnsley Junction and Penistone. This time, however, there were many fewer fatalities. *The Bristol Mercury* said that the accident had fortunately occurred near some farmhouses, so help could soon be obtained.

It happened between a coal train that had left Ardwick for Shire Oaks, near Sheffield, and an excursion train from Rotherham to Liverpool and Southport that left at 7.15 am. The excursion train had sixteen carriages and picked up a number of passengers at various stations.

The coal train suffered the same mishap as the engine in the previous Penistone accident when the axle broke on one of the coal trucks. The axle broke just as the trains passed on opposite lines and the broken wagon struck the engine of the passenger train. It bounced off the engine but then came back and hit the fourth carriage of the excursion train.

The coal truck smashed the carriage and the three following it. The coal train had been travelling at 15 miles an hour and the passenger train in the opposite direction at 25 miles an hour. *The Times*'s report claimed that blood was pouring upon the rails and it was extraordinary that anyone in the carriages remained alive. In fact, only four people died.

There were also a number of injured, some very badly. There was one elderly couple sitting together. As the carriage fell to pieces the man fell out of the carriage onto the lines and was killed. His wife stayed in her seat and was unharmed. It was only those sitting near the windows on the side of the train that was hit by the coal wagon that were hurt.

There was another case of decapitation between the last crash and the next one. It was reported in the *North-Eastern Daily Gazette* on 3 October 1885. The body of a young man with his head completely severed was found at 6.00 am in the Curb Tunnel on the London, Chatham and Dover Railway.

It was believed that the man had been killed the previous evening by the 10.30 pm train from Deal to Dover. When the train arrived at the destination a hat was found jammed in part of the engine. It seems that the tunnel was a

There were twenty-five deaths in the accident at Doncaster in 1887. Many of the victims were racegoers.

shortcut for people to get home at night, despite orders from the rail company against walking through it.

There was to be a two-year gap before the next fatal accident, which happened on 16 September 1887. It was, once again, on the Manchester, Sheffield and Lincolnshire Railway. This time the accident occurred between Hexthorpe Junction and Hexthorpe Bridge, about 2 miles from Doncaster.

Doncaster had been very full for a week due to the race meeting. Although many of the racegoers stayed in the town others were travelling in each day by train. As well as people, horses were also being brought in by train.

The Daily News of 17 September said that it had only been the previous day that the marvellous skill shown in dealing with the enormous rail traffic at the Doncaster races was the subject of deserved praise. It also mentioned that in the forty years since Doncaster had rail links with other large northern towns there had been no fatalities.

The Midland Railway race excursion train had been standing at the platform where the Hexthorpe Bridge crosses the line. Tickets were being collected and the guard had left his van to help with this. Then the Manchester, Sheffield and Lincolnshire railway train from Manchester ran into the back of it.

Almost all the injuries and damage were inflicted on the stationary train. The final three coaches, all Third Class, were smashed to pieces. There were twenty-five deaths and nearly a hundred injuries. Most of the fatalities were from the last three carriages. The driver, fireman and passengers on the Manchester train were almost entirely unhurt.

There seemed to be a fascination in the newspapers as to how miraculous some of the escapes from injury were. There was a baby taken alive from the arms of its dead mother. Others were uninjured despite being within a few feet of those who died instantly.

The Hexthorpe signalman and porters at the station said that the signals and flags were at danger against the Manchester train. It was thought that, due to either force of habit, inattention or difficulty of seeing them due to the rain, the driver ran past the signals.

An accident at Walthamstow in East London in 1887. Apart from the engine, much of the rest of the train has stayed on the line.

It was two years until the next serious fatal crash and it was once again on the Manchester, Sheffield and Lincolnshire Railway – again near Penistone and again due to a broken axle. The accident occurred on 30 March 1889.

The Times's report had noticed the connection and mentioned how Penistone had attained an evil notoriety through the frequency of serious mishaps in its vicinity. Surprisingly, this was not reflected in the headline of the story, which never mentioned Penistone at all.

The day was a busy one, with a number of special trains to London. This was for the FA Cup Final between Preston North End and Wolverhampton Wanderers and the Boat Race also taking place in London. One of these trains was a Manchester, Sheffield and Lincolnshire Railway train from Liverpool, which left at five minutes past midday.

The train had just passed Penistone Station and was near the Huddersfield Junction when the engine came off the rails. Officials of the railway agreed that this was once again due to a broken axle – the leading axle of the engine.

The mail train from King's Cross to Manchester was approaching and the driver and fireman from the derailed train managed to stop it as it approached the train blocking the line. A number of the carriages had buckled up against each other and were blocking the way of the King's Cross train.

There was only one death. It was thought that a passenger had jumped from the train when the carriages began to crash into each other and was then hit by one of the following carriages. There were, however, many injuries.

June 1889 was to see the biggest disaster so far in the number of deaths to have occurred on the railways in Britain. It even surpassed the Tay Bridge disaster in there being eighty deaths, many of them children. The disaster was not on the mainland but in Ireland, near Armagh Station.

The fact that the train was filled with families and children was shown in the report in the *North-Eastern Daily Gazette* on 13 June. The newspaper reported that a boy named Celeland, whose father, mother and two brothers died in the railway crash, had also died later at the county infirmary.

The accident happened on the lines of the Great Northern Railway Company of Ireland. The train involved was the annual excursion of Methodist Sunday school children between seven and sixteen years of age. It was organized by the pastor and the teachers. There were between 1,000 and 1,200 passengers on the train. The train was destined for Warren Point on Carlingford Bay and on the route there was a steep incline near Killooney that the train had to negotiate.

As the train began to climb the incline the engine seemed to be struggling to cope with the weight. Then part of the train broke free and began to run backwards down the slope. It seems that the couplings gave way under the strain. The first report said that following the excursion train was the normal 10.30 passenger train from Armagh. Another account in the same report said that the second train was part of the excursion, which had been split between two trains. This report said that the second train had stopped at Annaclare Bridge because it had gained on the first train.

The section of the first train and the second train collided and both of them fell off the embankment. This was 60 to 70 feet high at the point of the collision. The first report in *The Times* of 13 June gave the number of deaths as between sixty and seventy, mostly children. There were also many serious injuries.

The most serious accident to occur so far on Britain's railways was at Armagh in 1889, when a Sunday school outing train crashed.

The report in *The Times* the following day reverted to the opinion that the second train had in fact been a normal passenger train and not part of the excursion. It also gave the number of dead as eighty and said that the inquest had begun under Mr Peel, the coroner, in the Grand Jury Room.

The first matter dealt with by the inquest was the death of a Mr John Hughes, who had dropped dead from shock on seeing the scene of the disaster. Witnesses said that no one was near him when he just fell to the ground.

The stationmaster at Armagh Station said that just before the train left it was suggested that they attach a second engine to help pull the train up the incline. The engine driver had, however, claimed that one engine would be strong enough to do this.

One of the adult passengers, a Mrs Hamilton, the wife of a member of the Royal Irish Constabulary, said that when she saw the carriages moving backwards she began to throw children off the train before jumping off herself.

Another passenger, Mrs M'Combe, said that the train stopped and she was told that they did not have enough steam. Stones were put under the wheels of the rear carriages and the engine then moved off with the front carriages. This would suggest that the rear carriages were deliberately uncoupled rather than them having broken free. The report went on to state that the screams of the injured woman and children were enough to unnerve the strongest man – but there were very few men amongst the excursionists as they had mainly been women and children.

The Board of Trade report seemed to concentrate on the gradients of the line and had a number of diagrams of the area showing this. As well as a number of statements from the railway staff, it also included details of the deceased. It seems that, of the seventy-eight mentioned as dead, twenty-two were aged fifteen and under.

CHAPTER 9

1890 to 1900

Once the new decade had begun, it wasn't long before the first fatal accident. It happened on 4 March on the London and North Western Railway. An express train crashed into an engine at Carlisle, leading to four deaths and a number of injuries.

The Scottish express had left Euston at 8.00 pm and was due to reach Carlisle at 3.00 am. Those working in the station at Carlisle were surprised to see that the train was not slowing down as it reached the station. Thinking that this was due to the fact that it was late, they were not too worried at first. Instead of stopping, however, it sped through the station at 30 miles an hour and did not look like stopping at all.

It was evident that there was a problem with the brakes and this had stopped the train from slowing down. At that moment an engine was approaching from the north to take the train on to Glasgow and the train collided with it. The engine of the express stayed on the line but the first two carriages, a Third Class and a composite First and Third, were telescoped, the second one being driven halfway into the first. Three of the dead were thought to have been lying on the seats in their compartment. The driver and firemen of the engines survived.

The passengers on the Cape Mail steamer, *Norham Castle*, which arrived at Plymouth on 11 November 1890, may have safely come some distance aboard the ship from the Cape of Good Hope but they were not to make it much further after boarding their train.

The mail from the ship was sent on a special Post Office train run by the GWR. There were also forty-seven passengers who wanted to travel to London. A special train of three coaches was therefore sent with these passengers on board.

At Norton Fitzwarren, near Taunton, the engine of the special ran into the engine of a goods train that was stationary on the line. The drivers and firemen of both trains survived with slight injuries by jumping off before the

The Cape Mail Express was carrying passengers from a steamship that had arrived at Plymouth. It crashed at Norton Fitzwarren, near Taunton.

crash. The first carriage was badly damaged and then it caught fire, with a number of passengers trapped inside. Ten of them died.

The blame for the accident seemed to lie with a signalman, George Rice. The area where the accident took place was a busy junction with a number of different lines meeting. The goods train had been moved to its position to allow an express to pass. When the signalman was told about the special train he forgot about the goods train he had moved to the line and signalled all clear.

The Bury and Norwich Post obtained information about the accident from the Central News Telegram at 10.30 am, which at that time gave the number of dead as eight. The *North-Eastern Daily Gazette* had a local angle as they claimed that one of the injured came from Bishop Auckland.

The Board of Trade report stated that the accident was caused by the signalman at Norton Fitzwarren having forgotten about the down goods train that he had placed on the main up line. The report also mentioned how the GWR was constructing extensive new sidings that would stop the use of main lines as holding positions for waiting trains.

The Board of Trade report said that the goods trucks hit by the express were part of a train being shunted and one of the trucks had become derailed after a collision. There was some dispute as to the number of wagons that had been uncoupled during shunting but it was found that there had been no carelessness or breach of rules, so more rules were needed to ensure safety.

The decapitation of workers on the railway seemed to have happened on a number of occasions. It was rare for this to happen to a child but a case was reported in the *North-Eastern Daily Gazette* on 16 January 1892

Twelve-year-old Isabella Hogg of North Shields was killed on the Holywell Wagonway at Northumberland Dock. On her way home after attending a dinner with a man named Bainbridge, the girl was run over by some laden

Another view of the Cape Mail Express, showing the damage to the carriages.

wagons that were travelling down an incline towards the shipping staithes. It was reported that the body was mutilated in a dreadful manner and the face was unrecognizable. Her head had been detached and her chest was crushed. The remains were gathered with difficulty.

The next serious accident occurred on the Midland Railway on 9 June 1892. Five people died and a number were injured at Esholt Junction, about 10 miles from Leeds, when two trains collided. There was an interesting report in the *Belfast News-Letter,* which said the accident happened 6 miles from here, in Leeds. They had obviously copied the report from a newspaper much nearer Leeds. *The Birmingham Daily Post* had a more factual local basis when informing their readers that a Birmingham man, Sydney Smith, died in the accident.

The accident involved the 7.00 pm train from Leeds to Ilkley, which collided with the back of the 3.20 pm train from Ilkley to Bradford. The engine of the Leeds train hit the third carriage from the end of the Bradford train. The deaths and the worst injuries were all on the Bradford train.

The accident happened where the lines from Bradford and Leeds met. Just before the junction was a tunnel and the signal was just beyond this, which was against the Leeds train. The exit from the tunnel was through a wooded cutting and it was believed that the signal may have been obscured by foliage.

The end of June saw an interesting letter to *The Times* that showed it was not only people claiming damages from the railway companies. The letter was from a London solicitor who explained that one of his clients was driving a wagon across a weigh bridge belonging to a railway company. The bridge collapsed, causing the driver an injury.

The railway company then brought an action against the driver for the value of the bridge as they claimed the damage was caused by his negligence. The jury found against the company and the wagon driver had by then brought an action against the company for damages for his injuries. He was successful and was awarded £15. Being a relatively poor man, the wagon driver only employed a solicitor. The railway company employed a Queen's Counsel.

The railway company then appealed the decision three times, with one of the leaders of the Bar working for them. To support the wagon driver his solicitors had to also employ a Queen's Counsel. The result was that the driver ended up worse off because the cost of his case far outweighed the damages he had been awarded. The solicitor went on to claim that, with the wealth available to the railway companies, it was becoming one law for the rich and another for the poor.

There were ten deaths when two trains collided at Thirsk in November 1892. There was also a fire in the wreckage.

Another view of the wreckage at Thirsk. Fire was one of the greatest fears for those involved in an accident, especially if they were trapped.

There was another serious accident, on 2 November 1892, on the North Eastern Railway at Thirsk. Ten people died and many were injured when two trains collided. There was a fire and at first it was unclear how many had died. *The Bristol Mercury* headlined the story on the fire with: 'Train on fire – Terrible scenes'. This was another catastrophe, notwithstanding all the inventions of modern science.

The accident was caused by a mineral train being on the main line. The train came from Middlesbrough and entered the main line at Northallerton. From here it is 9 miles to Thirsk, where the train would normally leave the main line. It was, however, stopped at the signal at Manor House. While it was stopped at the signal, or shortly after moving off, the Scottish express ran into the back of it

There was, it seems, some blame attached to the signalman, who was then suspended from his job. There was much more to this story about the signalman, Mr Holmes, who worked from six in the evening until six in the morning. On the day previous to the accident he had finished work at 6.00 am. He was a young man with a family and after going to bed for a short time he was wakened because one of his children was ill. The child then died, so Holmes had had hardly any sleep.

A crash at Esholt Junction that happened in June 1892. The accident attracted some interested spectators.

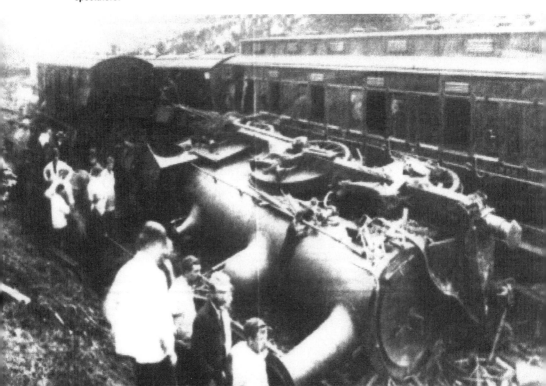

Holmes then asked if he could be excused from working that evening due to the death and the fact that he had had little sleep. It is hard to believe that his request was refused but he was told he had to work. No doubt at the time a person's employment was seen as more important than family life. It is hardly surprising then that grief and tiredness could have been responsible for his making a mistake.

It was not until August 1893 that the next serious accident occurred. It was on the Taff Valley Railway on 12 August at Llantrisant. There were thirteen people killed and a number of injuries when a train went down an embankment. There must have been much better worker benefits in Wales than in the rest of the country because, according to *The Birmingham Daily Post* of 14 August, many of the train's passengers were returning from a fortnight's holiday. Very few workers of the period would have had such long holidays. There were other people with plenty of leisure time, as the newspaper printed a report of a number of people who were nearly hit by falling carriages while blackberrying at the bottom of the embankment.

The 4.30 pm from Pontypridd to Cardiff comprised fifteen coaches and two vans. Four of the coaches belonged to the Cambrian Railway. It was one of these coaches that came off the line in the approach to Treforest Station. The driver noticed something was wrong but when he tried to stop the train he found that the engine had become uncoupled from the train.

The carriages then came off the rails and began to roll down the embankment, which was 60 to 70 feet high. They came to rest upside down in a field. There were soon many people at the site ready to help. One of the helpers was injured himself, and another died, although the circumstances were not reported in *The Times*.

By February 1893 the question of injury related to railway accidents and railway spine seemed to have become common knowledge, along with the question of the protagonists involved in such cases. There was a long report in *The Times* of 27 February 1893 that discussed a specific case and the problem in general.

The case was against the South Eastern Railway Company. The claimant had been shaken and hit his head during a collision in December 1890. The man went on to conduct his business with no problems until he got home. He then fell ill and after five months was sent into a hospital for the paralysed.

Doctors claimed that his spine had sustained a severe shock, which produced a weakness in the nerves connected to it. Although hoped for, his recovery was seen as uncertain. The report named his ailment as 'railway spine'. Doctors acting for the company claimed his symptoms were mental

The scene after a Scottish express ran into a coal train near Edinburgh. The weight of coal trains often caused such severe damage.

rather than physical. They believed that as soon as the case was settled his recovery would be rapid. They paid £200 into the court for him. The jury at the end of the trial awarded him another £650.

It seems that the railway company's representatives in court did not exert a good influence on the jury. They demanded that the defendant stand for cross examination rather than remain seated. The plaintiff was so disturbed that he broke down in court and had to lie on the floor to recover.

The report went on to describe the type of injuries that led to claims against railway companies. They described the claimants as often having been shaken about but having no external injury. There were quotes from surgical textbooks calling this type of injury railway spine. The report then went on to support the railway company claim by saying that, in many cases, recovery was instant after the damages claim was settled.

The Times's report did not claim that in these cases there had been a deliberate attempt to mislead the court but did say that suffering was sometimes exaggerated. Evidence was mainly based on the statement of the patient and it was hard to tell the extent of the truth in this. This could be because the patient of a nervous disposition may easily persuade himself of the reality of his condition. The writer would seem to have been reading *Page's Railway Injuries* book.

The Times went on to say that railway companies had been victimized in some cases by ingenious malingering. It therefore was the duty of the directors to investigate all demands, even at the risk of punishing the innocent for the guilty. There had been an instance where so many claims had been brought under the direction of the same doctor that the company laid charges of conspiracy against him and one of his patients. The doctor was not convicted.

The story went on to say how such damages cases became an arena for battle between rival experts whose eagerness to triumph over each other made them oblivious of anything else. In these cases the judge had to exalt the claims of common sense above scientific knowledge. They then let the jury decide for themselves when doctors disagreed.

A large crowd gathers to watch the clearing of the wreckage after an accident at Northallerton in 1894.

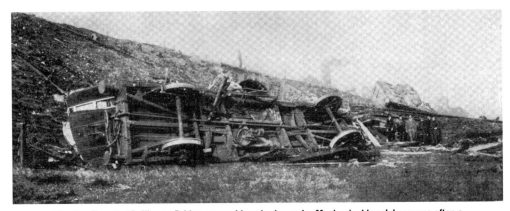

The derailment at Bullhouse Bridge, caused by a broken axle. Mechanical breakdown was often a cause of accidents.

The Chelford accident, caused by a train running into a loose goods wagon on the line.

The report did state that claims against railway companies had been decreasing. This may have been due to attempts by the company medical assessors to visit the victim and settle out of court – a method that the Lord Chief Justice was not happy about, especially when it took place during a trial.

Accidents at Christmas time had occurred over the years and there was to be another in 1894. This was on 22 December on the London and North Western Railway at Chelford. There were fourteen people killed and a number of injured. The trains on Saturdays close to Christmas would have always been very busy.

The Manchester to London express had left on time and was indeed very busy. The front carriages of the train were bound for Birmingham and the rest for London. Because of the number of passengers and the size of the train it was pulled by two engines.

The train was travelling at around 60 miles an hour when it reached Chelford. Here it seemed that some goods wagons had been blown onto the track due to a storm and the express smashed into them. It resulted in fourteen deaths and numerous injuries. This was mainly amongst those in the Birmingham carriages.

There was a serious accident on the Great Northern Line in November 1895. It was similar to a previous accident in that it involved the London to Scotland express and a coal train. This time, however, the coal train was on the correct line. The train had left King's Cross at 11.30 pm and had reached St Neot's in Huntingdonshire during the night. Just before the station a rail broke and one of the carriages on the express came off the rails and hit a coal wagon that was stationary in a siding. The carriage and the two following it were all badly damaged.

The rest of the train carried on but when it was stopped it was found that a number of the carriages still attached to the engine were also slightly damaged. There was only one fatality, a 15-year-old girl, but a number of other passengers were seriously injured.

Sir Henry Oakley, general manager of the GNR, said the train had consisted of nine coaches, including a Pullman car. It was being pulled by one of the new powerful engines. There had only been twenty-seven passengers. He went on to explain that the accident was due to a broken rail. The break was new and bright and there was no indication of a previous fault. Another official of the company stated that the break in the rail had been caused by the engine. The high rate of speed and the lightness of the coupling carried the first carriage and the Pullman car across the break.

There was an inquiry, attended by Mr W.L. Jackson MP, chairman of the

A derailed engine surrounded by a crowd of men. The location is not indentified but it is obviously a carefully posed image.

GNR. Sir Henry Oakley, general manager, and Mr F. Cockshot, superintendent of the line. The broken rail had previously been inspected, with no sign of a problem. The train had been travelling at about 60 miles an hour when the rail broke into several pieces.

The next serious accident that happened, on 6 April 1896, was unusual in that it occurred on the first official opening trip of a new railway. This was the Snowdon Mountain Railway. There had been a number of preliminary trips for the press and locals before the line opened officially.

The railway had been certified for traffic by the Board of Trade. There was no ceremonial opening of the line and the first trip was under way. One of the most critical parts of the journey was about halfway between the terminal stations. This was on an embankment with a very sharp curve.

Two trains carrying about a hundred passengers had made the trip upwards with no problems. The trip back down was to be a disaster. The engine of the first train got out of gear, came off the line, fell about 100 feet and was smashed to pieces. The driver and fireman managed to jump off before the engine went over the edge.

The wreckage of a carriage at New Cross, London, where three people died. One can only imagine what it must have been like inside the carriage at the moment of impact.

The carriages would have seemed to be in danger of following the engine over the edge, but the railway did not couple the trains. Each carriage had a strong brake. The manager of the railway applied the brake and shouted at the passengers not to jump off. Some did and it was amongst these that the worst injuries occurred. One of the injured later died.

When the first engine fell it damaged the telegraph system so that a bell rang at the summit telling the second train to descend. Although attempts were made to stop the second train, thick fog made this impossible and it crashed into the two stationary carriages. Thankfully, the passengers had already climbed out before the carriages were sent over the edge of the embankment.

There was a short period without any serious fatal crashes or other train-related accidents. Between the last and next fatal accident, however, there were some serious accidents on viaduct construction. Twelve men died on 9 February 1897 at the Coldrennick Viaduct when a platform fell. Then two men died in an accident during building work at Trevido Viaduct. Both viaducts were near Menheniot Station in Cornwall.

The next serious accident on the railways was on the Cambrian Railway at Welshampton on 11 June 1897. This was another Sunday school excursion,

The train at Heathfield has fallen down a high embankment in this 1898 accident.

There is a large amount of wreckage but little damage to the engine in this photograph of an unidentified accident.

from Royton, near Oldham, to Barmouth in West Wales. According to *The Morning Post* of 14 June the passengers were members of the St Paul's Sunday School of Royton, near Oldham, on their annual excursion.

The train was on its return journey, with fifteen coaches and two engines. There were about 300 passengers. At Welshampton the wheels of one of the tenders came off the rails. One of the engines and thirteen coaches then also came off the rails. Some of the coaches were telescoped into each other. There were a number of injuries and eleven deaths.

The cause is thought to have been due to a Third Class brake coach that belonged to the Lancashire and Yorkshire railway leaving the track. The coach was a light one with only four wheels. All the other coaches were heavy composite coaches with three or four pairs of wheels. The coupling attached to the next coach had snapped.

A familiar name was involved in a fatal accident on 10 October 1897. It was at Penistone, where fatal accidents had occurred a few years before. This time there was one death, at Penistone Station.

The accident involved the 5.00 pm express from London. The engine and four coaches were detached from the train and moved to the down line. This was to allow a carriage to be uncoupled for another train. The carriage when it was uncoupled ran back down the line, which was on a gradient, and it hit an engine that had come to take it away for the Lancashire and Yorkshire Railway.

There were five injuries, and one of the injured died. A government inspector said that the blame was due to a porter named Haigh, who had unhooked the carriage before the engine to take it had returned to it. He did not, however, believe there was any deliberate intent on the porter's part in what happened.

As the century drew towards its end the final two serious accidents were to occur in 1898. The first was at Wellingborough, on the Midland Railway, on 2 September, when there were seven deaths and more than sixty injuries caused by a small trolley. The train was described as all in a heap after the collision.

The accident was caused by a luggage trolley that fell off the platform onto the rails. It then caused a train to be derailed. One witness said that as the truck was being pulled along the platform there was a group of small boys jumping on and off the trolley. The witness had turned away and when he turned back the trolley was on the line. There was some suspicion that the boys may have pushed it onto the line deliberately. One of the boys, a 10-year-old, was interviewed and had been employed by a local newsagent. He had gone to the station to get some newspapers and was actually helping to push the trolley.

The last serious accident of the century took place at Wrawby Junction on 17 October 1898. It was on the Great Central Railway. It involved the 4.45 pm train from Cleethorpes to Manchester. There were eight deaths and a number of injuries.

The accident was caused when the Manchester train passed Wrawby Junction and some of the carriages struck timber on a goods train on an

The wreckage of a train at Wellingborough Station that had run into a luggage trolley that was on the line. It is amazing that such a small item could cause so much damage.

adjacent line. The timber caught the top of the carriages and lifted them off. Most of the other carriages were undamaged.

The Times's report stated that thousands of people gathered in the area once the news of the accident became known. This attraction to viewing serious accidents seems to have been a regular phenomenon and the crowd cannot in this case have been due to the gathering of those worried about relatives and friends.

CHAPTER 10

1900 to 1914

The new century was not very old before the first fatal rail crash occurred. It was on the North British Railway on 28 March, between Glasgow and Helensburgh. *The Times*'s report stated that the area was a busy system with workers from the East End of Glasgow travelling out to the factories on the banks of the Clyde. The two trains involved were mainly filled with workers from the Singer factory at Kilbowie.

The *Aberdeen Weekly Journal* described the trains as 'workmen's trains'.

A badly damaged engine with what looks like a young girl nearby. It seems that anyone could get close to rail accidents in the past.

Their report said that two trains collided at Charing Cross Station, Glasgow, and that two were killed on the spot and three of the injured died later.

The accident involved a collision in a tunnel. The first train had left Queen Street Station at about 6.00 am and reached the tunnel about a mile past the station. It stopped in the tunnel due to an accident, according to *The Times*. However, according to the *Aberdeen Weekly Journal* the train stopped because of a problem with the Westinghouse braking system. The second train was due to leave the station fifteen minutes later but should not have been allowed to leave until the line was clear.

There was no possibility of the second train stopping as it only saw the rear light of the first train at the last moment. The casualties were confined to the final three carriages of the first train. The fact that the accident occurred in the darkness of the tunnel made rescue more difficult. Seven people died.

The signalman at Charing Cross, James Rintoul, seemed to have signalled that the line was clear without having seen the first train pass. He was arrested and taken to the police station. The *Aberdeen Weekly Journal* stated that the Queen Street signalman had been told by the Charing Cross signalman that the line was clear.

There were only a few more months before the second fatal accident of the year occurred, this time on the Great Western Railway at Slough, on 16 June. The Windsor train arrived at Slough Station at about 1.30 pm and stopped while passengers departed. A few minutes later, the West of England Express approached at full speed on the same line.

A porter tried to signal the express to stop and, after being warned, many of the passengers on the stationary train managed to get off before the collision. When the express struck, the rear carriages of the stationary train rose up and damaged the station roof and the footbridge over the lines. Some of the carriages then caught fire.

The dead numbered five passengers from those who were on the stationary train, and the driver and fireman of the express were badly injured. The local fire brigade arrived to put out the fire and the police were there to hold back the crowd. *The Times* reported that these were people worried about friends and family on the trains but I suspect that, as with other railway accidents, many were just there to take a look at the accident.

The Times's report went on to say that the directors of the GWR were reluctant to express any opinion as to why the express had passed the danger signals at the station. This was in view of the expected Board of Trade inquiry, which was to follow.

The accident was also reported in the *Belfast News-Letter* of 18 June. It

GRETNA RAILWAY ACCIDENT. MAY 1901.
RAISING THE ENGINE.

An accident at Gretna in 1901. The raising of the engine has attracted a lot of spectators. Whatever is pulling the engine is out of the frame of the photograph.

was very similar to *The Times*'s report and had come from a 'Special correspondent of the Press Association'.

There were a few years of relative safety on the railways before another serious accident, in Glasgow, on the 27 July 1903. According to *The Times* of 28 July, it was one of the most disastrous accidents in the history of the railways in Scotland. There were fifteen deaths and a number of injuries. *The Manchester Guardian* of 28 July declared it the worst accident to have happened in Scotland since the Tay Bridge disaster.

The accident occurred at St Enoch Station and involved only one train. The station had recently been extended and some of the platforms were quite short. The platform where the accident occurred was also around a sharp bend. The train was a connection with a steamer from the Isle of Man. It was supposedly full of working-class holidaymakers who had been spending a week on the island.

The damaged engine of the 1903 Waterloo disaster. Another accident that occurred in a station.

The Guardian went into the details of the situation and said that for the past few years the fair holiday in Glasgow for artisans and the working class had passed without mishap despite the amount of traffic at its end and beginning. The amount of traffic was abnormal and had taxed the upmost resources of the railway companies. It was obviously to prove too much in this case.

The tickets were collected about a half a mile from the terminus and after that many of the passengers were standing up in the carriages, collecting luggage. The engine could not stop in time and hit the station buffers at a high speed. The main damage was to the first two carriages, where the majority of the casualties were.

There were fifteen deaths, which seems excessive given that it was simply a case of the train hitting the buffers. Carriages telescoping into each, however, points to a serious problem with railway carriages at this time, and it seems to have been a regular occurrence. The weakness of carriages was the main problem as the driver was in the first vehicle to hit the buffers and was unhurt. He was what was known as a spare man, or normally a goods train driver, and he blamed the brakes for failing. He was arrested and held in custody.

Railway accidents at Christmas time continued in 1904. Two days before Christmas there was an accident at Aylesbury involving a mail train, in which four men died. On Christmas Eve *The Times* reported there had been three deaths but this was based on a statement from the Great Central Railway.

According to the GCR's statement to the newspaper, the mail train left the lines at Aylesbury Junction at 3.45 am. The train's fireman, and a fireman and driver travelling as passengers, died and the driver of the train was seriously injured. Another train, the up mail, also hit the wreckage of the derailed train but no one on this train was injured. There were no passengers on the derailed train apart from the two men already mentioned. There was also a guard and a dining room attendant, who were not badly hurt.

The Manchester Guardian report of the same day was very similar. It said that the newspaper train had run off the tracks at Aylesbury and, while the wreckage was obstructing the line, a train from Manchester had run into it. The report had a steament from the Press Association saying that if the train had been full of passengers it would have been too appalling to think about.

The wreck of the Cromer Express at Witham, in Essex, in 1905. Apart from ten passengers who were killed, a porter was also killed on the platform.

The scene of the Salisbury disaster in 1906, showing the wreck of the train in the station.

A closer view of the wreckage of the Salisbury disaster of 1906. The person who sent this card was working on the wreckage and said that it was very hard work.

The train had come off the rails on a bend where there was a speed limit of 15 miles an hour. The approaching train managed to slow down before it hit the wreckage and so there was little further damage.

There was a strange report in *The Times* on 20 January 1905, stating: 'The appalling railway accident that occurred on the Midland line yesterday must rank among the graver disasters from which we in this country are comparatively free.' I'm not sure why the writer thought this. There were seven deaths in the accident, which occurred at Cudworth, South Yorkshire. It had only been eighteen months since twice this number had died in another accident.

A mail train from Leeds to Sheffield was hit by the Scottish express going to London, which was travelling at a much faster pace than the mail train. Both trains were reported as wrecked and on fire. There had at this time been six deaths but it was stated that people were trapped.

There was snow on the ground and it was foggy so it was difficult to find anyone trapped in the wreckage. It was thought that the fog had come down very quickly and that may have been why the express driver had not seen any danger signals. There was a hint that perhaps the driver had not looked but the report said it was too early to say whether this was true.

There was a change in the reporting of accidents in the early twentieth century. There had for many years been drawings of accidents in such newspapers as the *The Illustrated London News*. By this time other newspapers such as *The Penny Illustrated Paper* were using photographs.

Photographs of the Cudworth accident appeared in *The Penny Illustrated Paper* but not until 28 January. They published photographs of rescue workers moving the dead and injured from the wreckage. The captions mentioned how the wreckage was burning due to the gas main of the express having burst.

The accident that happened on 27 July 1905, halfway between Liverpool and Southport, was unusual in that one of the trains was electric-powered. The line had recently been electrified. The electric train had been in a siding at Hall Road Station when an express from Liverpool ran into it. According to *The Times*, a Liverpool architect saw what was about to happen and told the passengers in the express to lie on the floor. This reduced injuries on the express but twenty people died on the electric train.

Crowds were reported at Southport Station waiting for news of the accident. There were also thousands of people assembled on the golf links opposite where the accident happened. *The Times*'s report didn't say that these people were all worried about friends and family on the trains. A crowd of

The Grantham disaster of September 1906. There were not many people at the scene when this photograph was taken.

that many must have been there out of interest in the accident and people were known to take souvenirs such as parts of the train.

It was thought that a problem with the points may have sent the express onto the siding rather than keeping it on the main line. The passenger superintendent of the line, Mr Nicholson, said he had no idea how the accident happened.

The Manchester Guardian report of 28 July concentrated more on the electric line than the accident. The newspaper seemed to be very interested in explaining how things were and informing their readers about the background information of such an event rather than the event itself.

The report explained that since the line had been electrified a year earlier, the number of trains between Liverpool and Southport had increased, as had their speed. It was one of the few electrified lines in the country and there had been a number of small mishaps where fires had started due to electrification. Commenting on the accident it said that the wreckage had caught fire due to the electric current in the live rail.

The Board of Trade report had lists of the type of vehicles that made up

RAILWAY SMASH GRANTHAM 19.9.06

Another view of the accident at Grantham, with some police officers and a fireman. The train was supposed to stop at the station but went straight through.

the trains. There were a number of eight-wheeled vehicles. There were statements from all the signalmen involved, the majority of them being very experienced, with more than twenty years' service. The accident was caused, according to the report, by a breach of the block system by either a signalman or the driver of an express, and it was mainly the duty of the driver, not the fireman, to view the signals.

The year 1905 was turning out to be the worst for rail accidents for some time. The third serious accident of the year occurred on 1 September in Essex. It involved the Cromer Express from Liverpool Street on the Great Eastern Railway.

The train had reached Witham, which was the branch line junction for Braintree and Maldon. As it passed through the station the third carriage broke free. The engine and the first two carriages carried on, while the remaining carriages began to disintegrate. One mounted the platform, another caught fire. Four carriages were badly damaged.

The ten deaths all occurred in one of the carriages that mounted the platform. The carriage also destroyed a porter's hut and killed one of the porters, who was inside. The last four carriages were undamaged. One of these was filled with children from Dr Barnado's homes bound for Felixstowe. None of them were hurt.

Not all of the children on the train escaped unhurt, however. *The Times*'s report stated that a girl of seven broke her arm and had her scalp removed. While the doctor was sewing her head, she said, 'If you do that again I'll tell my mummy.' She then apparently fell asleep without knowing that her mother had died.

The Manchester Guardian was obviously worried that its readers may not know where Witham was, so they explained that it was 39 miles from London and 9 miles north of Chelmsford. They thought that the axle may have broken, causing the carriage to come off the rails.

There could have been greater disaster had the accident happened earlier, as the Cromer to Liverpool Street train would have passed and hit the wreckage. There was also a fire due to the gasometers under the carriages being ruptured. *The Guardian* report also mentioned a passenger from Ilford who had earlier moved from the damaged carriage because it had been too crowded.

The Witham crash was the last serious rail accident of the year but it was not the last instance of railway related deaths. On 5 December the roof of Charing Cross Station in London collapsed, killing six people.

The year 1905 had been a bad one for the railways, but 1906 was to be

A small engine derailed at Murthwaite in Cumbria.

even worse. This was despite the first six months being relatively clear of serious accidents. The first one took place on 30 June at Salisbury, on the London and South Western Railway. There were twenty-eight deaths, the highest number for some years.

The train involved was a special from Plymouth to London. It was carrying passengers from the steamship *New York* from America and many of those who died were American. For some unknown reason the train came off the rails at Salisbury Station. It was a small train, with only three First Class carriages.

The engine of the express then hit a milk train on the other line, instantly killing the driver of the milk train. This collision stopped the express from falling down the embankment onto the street below. One carriage hit a bridge and part of this and one of the passengers was thrown onto the street below.

The Times's report went on to describe some of the personal tragedies. One family with five children all died, except the father. Another couple were on their honeymoon; the woman escaped unhurt but her new husband died. This was described in the report as the most pathetic feature of the accident – obviously more so, they thought, than the deaths of the children.

The rail industry employed a huge number of men in the early nineteenth century, as shown in this view of staff leaving the Swindon works.

As with many accidents there were some lucky escapes. Many of the passengers on the steamship had decided to carry on their boat trip to Southampton. This included the mayor of New York, Mr G.B. McClellan. Their train from Southampton arrived safely at Waterloo.

The Penny Illustrated Paper published photographs of the accident a week after it happened. They also explained that half the passengers on the train were killed instantly – a very high percentage of fatalities even if there were not many of them.

The Board of Trade report described how the train had been a small one with eight-wheeled carriages. It was a regular Saturday timetable for the American steam ship arriving at Plymouth.

There had been a problem with how the train had approached Salisbury Station, according to the report. Since April 1904 there had been a speed limit of 30 miles per hour for any train passing through and not stopping at the station. The guard on the train said that the driver did not apply his brakes as they approached. They were actually travelling at between 50 to 60 miles an hour when the collision took place. The guard had even applied his own brakes gently to remind the driver, but this did not work and there was not enough brake power to affect the train's speed.

The next accident of the year occurred on 19 September and news of it had only just arrived in London in time for a few particulars to be published in *The Times*'s report of the 20th. It involved the 8.45 pm train from King's Cross to Scotland. The train was supposed to stop at Grantham but reports state that it went through the station at 40 miles an hour.

Because it was supposed to stop, the points were set for another line. This stretch of line was supposed to be traversed at no more than 9 miles an hour. The train came off the line and hit a wall. There were thirteen deaths. This included the driver and the fireman, so asking them for an explanation of why the train did not stop was not possible.

An interesting card showingf the Woodhouse Junction crash near Sheffield. As well as a number of views there are photographs of the guard, fireman and driver.

The Tonbridge disaster of 1909. The scene is unusual in that there is a fence along the railway.

The Times did mange to find some consolation for the deceased in that the majority of them died instantly or, as the reporter put it, 'merciful in their suddenness'. There was according to the report a relief from the horror with an almost comical escape. This involved the guard climbing out of the window of his van, but I fail to see the humour in that.

Once again, *The Penny Illustrated Paper* printed a series of photographs of the Grantham accident. There was no story, for some reason, just a headline, 'After the catastrophe', as well as a series of photographs. These appeared a week after the accident.

The last serious accident of 1906 occurred a few days after Christmas, on 28 December, at Elliot Junction near Arbroath. The railway lines in the area had been blocked by snow for the previous twenty-four hours but the line between Dundee and Arbroath had reopened. This turned out to be unfortunate for the twenty-two victims who died.

The train had stopped at a signal at Elliot Junction to see if the line was clear. It was then struck from behind by an express train on the North British Railway. The guard's van and the rear carriage, full of storm-stayed passengers, were smashed to pieces.

The driver of the express, George Gourlay, later said that he was running at 20 miles an hour and all the signals showed that the line was clear. The driver had hit his head and suffered a bad cut. He was shocked by the accident and did not even know what had happened to the young fireman, Irvine, who had been with him on the footplate. The fireman was one of the dead.

The Penny Illustrated Paper published a report a week after the accident. It explained that the express got as far as Arbroath but could get no further. The engine was then swapped to the other end of the train and it was to return the way it had come. It then hit the other train.

After two bad years, 1907 turned out to be much safer for rail travellers. The only serious accident of the year occurred on 15 October, at Shrewsbury, and resulted in eighteen deaths. This was obviously a shock as there had been the worst accident for some time at the same place the year before. This accident was similar to the earlier one in that the train left the line. According to *The Times* of 16 October, this was because the driver was trying to make up time and went too fast over what should have been a stretch of slow line. As the driver died, there was no proof of this.

The disaster at Elliot Junction of December 1906. One train ran into another that was standing in the station.

This view of the Shrewsbury accident of 1907 was printed on an enormous postcard. Rail crashes were a favourite topic for postcards.

The train was a joint London and North Western and Great Western Railway Bristol express. The powerful LNW engine left the tracks and fell over. The weight of the following carriages pushed the first carriage up onto the engine. The report stated that at some points the wreckage was 30 feet high.

According to Mr Baxter, the chief constable of Shrewsbury, two of his officers witnessed the accident. They said that the train was going very fast and had passed a danger signal at Crewe Bank. It then struck one of the sets of points, which were set against it due to the danger signal. The engine was a new one, weighing 100 tons, which then stopped the carriages, forcing them to telescope.

The Penny Illustrated Paper published interviews with eyewitnesses. Mr Allen from Liverpool described his escape from the accident as miraculous but his memory was still dazed and imperfect so he didn't describe the escape. There was another witness who said that the accident resulted in an indescribable scene of horror. As it couldn't be described, the newspaper published photographs of it instead.

The accident at Shrewsbury was to be the last serious rail accident for some time. There were none at all in 1908 involving train crashes or derailments. However, a report entitled 'Railway Accidents in 1908' appeared in *The Times*. It was based on the return of accidents and casualties as reported to the Board of Trade.

The report gave the number of killed during the year as 1,043, with 7,984 injured. Of these, 479 were killed due to trespass, including suicides. Other causes led to 102 deaths of passengers, and 376 railway servants were killed by other causes. Fifty-one people were killed passing over level crossings. There were twenty-nine killed while on business at stations or other causes not mentioned.

The numbers for 1908 were compared with the previous year and were very similar apart from those killed in railway accidents in 1907. It would seem then that deaths due to train crashes and derailments were a minority of the deaths that occurred on the railways. Many of the type of deaths not connected with rail accidents would not be reported widely. There is no reason to suspect that these figures for these two years were very different from other years.

After a quite long spell without any serious rail accidents the next one occurred on 29 January 1910. *The Times's* reports were quick to mention this spell of grace and the first line of their report of 31 January said, 'The immunity from serious mishap which English railways have enjoyed came to an end on Saturday.'

The accident happened on the London, Brighton and South Coast Railway when the Brighton express to Victoria reached Stoat's Nest Station and one of the Third Class carriages came off the tracks. The coupling snapped and the carriage crashed onto the station platform. The engine and coaches still attached stayed on the line. Those behind the broken carriage came off the line but stayed upright and were hardly damaged.

The serious injuries and seven deaths all occurred in the Third Class carriage that had mounted the platform. It later became clear that only six of the dead were passengers on the train. The seventh was a man who had been walking along the platform and had been hit by the carriage. As with other accidents that attracted crowds of sightseers there were, according to *The Times's* report, a number of photographers who were stationed on a nearby hill, and their dazzling flashlights hampered those involved in rescue work.

There was a report in *The Manchester Guardian* that showed a glimpse of the humour that the newspaper was to become famous for. The headline of *The Guardian* report described it as 'A weird scene of wreckage'. Darkness had fallen soon after the accident occurred. Due to this the breakdown gang were seriously handicapped when trying to use a steam crane. All the work had to be done using artificial light. This was supplied by large flare jets known as 'Lucy Janes'. The report explained that at midnight the railway officials were still 'in the dark' as to the reason for the accident.

The next accident occurred at the end of the year and was another Christmas catastrophe. It happened on Christmas Eve 1910, at Hawes Junction near Carlisle, and led to twelve deaths. An express from London had hit two engines, causing the telescoping of two of the carriages.

That Christmas of 1910 was not a very happy one. The report of the Hawes Junction crash in *The Times* also mentioned an accident at Chesterfield, where a train had hit a number of children, killing three of them, as well as a mining disaster in Pretoria in which 300 had died.

Although a number of the passengers died instantly at Hawes Junction, others were killed by the resulting fire in the damaged carriages. *The Times* declared that in some aspects the accident had no parallel in the history of rail travel in this country. The train was full of exiles from the north going home for Christmas.

The express came out of a tunnel and was travelling at about 65 miles an hour when the driver saw two engines on the line travelling in the same direction but at a slower pace. Although they applied the brakes there was no chance of avoiding the collision.

The train caught fire and this spread along the carriages. It was dark and raining hard and the site of the crash was desolate with only a few cottages, the nearest town, Hawes, being 6 miles away. Another engine arrived on the scene and its water was used to attempt to put the fires out but this was unsuccessful.

The report explained how the few rescuers there tried to free one man who was trapped but they were eventually driven back by the flames. They could hear the man screaming until he eventually went quiet.

The first seven coaches were destroyed by fire. *The Times*'s reporter arrived the next day and said that normally at a rail crash there were articles heaped on the line. This scene was just a mass of wheels as the rest of the carriages had been burnt.

The accident had apparently occurred because the signalman had sent the two engines onto the main line. He had then forgotten about them and could not see them due to the bad weather. The express was then sent onto what he thought was a clear line.

The Observer of Christmas Day also described other Christmas disasters.

A cartoon from 1911 shows that despite railway staff working hours and wages being settled, safety was still a big issue.

There had been three train crashes in France and one in America within the past few days. Describing the Hawes accident the paper stated that the bodies of the victims were charred beyond recognition.

The Observer's headlines were quite horrific; one described how a baby was killed before its parents' eyes, but in the main body of the story the nephew of General Sir Archibald Hunter, who had minor injuries, was mentioned before the story of the dead baby. The child was reported to have been consumed by fire.

Railway officials made a statement that seemed to go against the report in *The Times* about how a man was trapped and then burnt to death. They claimed that the fatalities were killed outright and were burnt afterwards.

The next serious accident occurred only a month after the last one. This time it was in Wales, on the Taff Vale Railway near Pontypridd Junction. A passenger train carrying 200 passengers collided with a mineral train on the same line. There were eleven deaths. There was help on hand for the injured from the Metropolitan Police and soldiers who were stationed in the Rhondda Valley in case of disturbances from the men on strike in the Cambrian Colliery. Three of the dead were important members of the Welsh Miners' Federation.

There were about sixty police officers and fifty soldiers who had been used in the past few months to control rioting by striking miners. They were based at Pontypridd and came from the barracks there to help. Local opinion had it that more trouble had broken out when the miners saw them leave their quarters.

The passenger train was running from Swansea to Cardiff. The first carriages of the train telescoped when the engine struck the coal train. It was in these carriages that the fatalities occurred. The coal train was also bound towards Cardiff but was stationary, waiting for a signal to allow it to move. The cause seems to have either been a mistake by the signalman or that the driver of the passenger train passed a danger signal.

The report in *The Manchester Guardian* described the accident as similar to the disaster at Hawes Junction the month before. It was similar in that one train crashed into the back of another due to some problems with signalling.

The Guardian report filled in the background of the area. The soldiers who aided the victims were from the West Riding Regiment and the event occurred near the Great Western Colliery, where sixty men had died a few years before. The report described how the conference of the Federation of Miners of Great Britain that took place in London was overshadowed by the death of three of its members in the accident.

There was some respite from serious accidents for nearly two years. It seems that, apart from 1905 and 1906, the number of serious accidents had declined in recent years although the number of fatalities was often higher than in accidents of the distant past.

There was an accident at Wombwell on the Great Central Railway on 13 December 1911, which resulted in two deaths. It involved a coal train from Sheffield to Wath Yard and seven wagons that were being shunted near the main signal box.

The coal train had gone out of control and was travelling down an incline between Rockingham South signal box and Wombwell Station. It passed several danger signals. It was a large train of forty-four loaded wagons and twelve empty ones. It was travelling very fast when it hit the wagons being shunted by an engine.

The Wombwell accident of 13 December 1911. The wreckage shows how powerful the accident must have been. This was caused by a runaway train.

Another view of the Wombwell crash. The engine appears to have survived much better than the trucks.

The engine of the coal train overturned, killing the fireman instantly, and the driver died before he could be released from the wreckage. It seems that there was inadequate brake power to stop the train as it ran down the incline.

The next serious accident happened on 17 September 1912, in Lancashire. There were fifteen deaths. It happened on the London and North Western Railway at Ditton Junction near Widnes. The train was the 5.30 pm train from Chester to Liverpool. The engine came off the rails going down an incline and hit a bridge. The carriages then broke free and ran into a platform. Some were smashed to pieces while others caught fire. The fireman was trapped under the overturned engine for more than three hours but thankfully the engine was clear of the burning carriages. Incidents of fires in accidents seemed to be becoming more frequent at this time, perhaps due to the use of gas lighting in railway carriages.

The Times's report described how capricious the effects of the accident were. A horse in a horsebox that was smashed to pieces survived while a horse in another horsebox that was hardly damaged died. A young girl trapped under a carriage was released unharmed while many around her were dismembered.

The Manchester Guardian report went into more detail. The train had passed over a bridge across the river Mersey before it went down the incline. After the accident hundreds of men were using feverish energy to release the dead and dying. Waiting rooms on the platforms of the station had been turned into makeshift hospitals.

There were some more personal reports, such as that of the man bent over his dead wife at the station. Blood was still flowing from his own wounds. The couple had been on their way to Southport for two weeks' holiday. Another of those who died was a woman described as having her arms across her face as though shielding herself from the fire.

The Board of Trade report was written by Lieutenant Colonel H.A. Yorke. He described the accident as the worst since the one at Shrewsbury in 1907, and in some respects quite similar. There was, he said, no previous record of an accident where the engine had broken its back or there had been such destruction of rolling stock. Despite there being three hydrants in the station and a good supply of water, it had been difficult to control the fire that had

The engine after the crash at Ditton Junction in 1912. Fifteen died in the accident.

An accident at Manchester in 1912. It is hard to see from the photograph what exactly happened.

broken out. Men from the company sleeper works nearby had come to help.

There was a serious accident at Colchester on 12 June 1913, on the Eastern Counties Railway, in which three men died. *The Observer* of 13 July reported that the train came round a slight curve and ran into a light engine that was taking on water. It was not explained why the engine was on the line. The following day, *The Guardian* repeated a similar story and said that by some oversight, which was not explained, a light engine was left standing on the line.

The inquest was held at Colchester Town Hall on 14 July under the borough coroner, Mr H. Geoffrey Elwes. Unlike early inquests when the victims were rarely represented, a solicitor appeared for the Society of Locomotive Engineers, for Sidney Keeble, the fireman, and another for the National Union of Railwaymen, for William Barnard, the driver, and Burnett, the guard. There were also representatives of the NUR and ASLEF. William Barnard's father had also died in a railway accident in 1900 when the engine he was on blew up.

The inquiry found that the signalman Kerry had put up a danger signal when the light engine came to a halt, which was correct. He then, however, sent the 'train out of section' signal to the junction signal box. This should only have been done when the engine was moving or clear of the main line.

It seems that Kerry normally used the train out of section signal and believed that the danger signal was enough of a warning. The chairman of the GER later decided that Kerry could not return to work for the company. Despite the fact that he had worked for the company for twenty-nine years they would not change their decision, even after representation from the union.

The Observer mentioned that there had been some local dissatisfaction at the dismissal of signalman Kerry on 27 July. A driver and fireman had apparently refused duty because of the matter. Kerry was prominent in local politics and had stood, unsuccessfully, for the local council in Colchester.

Scottish express trains seem to be overrepresented in serious accidents. There was another on 1 September 1913. It happened on the Midland Railway at Hawes Junction, close to the site of a previous accident of December 1910. The cause was also similar, one train running into another, although this time two express trains were involved.

The first train had stopped at the highest point on the line for want of steam. There was a lot of telescoping after the collision and, as in the last accident on that spot, the trains caught fire. The number of deaths was also similar, fourteen in this crash, twelve in the previous one.

The inquest was to be held under Major Pringle, who had held the inquest for the last crash. The dead had not been identified due to the burnt condition of the bodies. One of the injured was, however, named as Sir Arthur Douglas, former undersecretary for defence in New Zealand.

At normal times there would only have been one express running. However, due to it being holiday time, two express trains were running. There was only a twelve-minute gap between the two trains leaving Carlisle.

The Manchester Guardian report went into more detail about the problems on the railway rather than just about the accident itself. Again, the driver had run past a signal at danger. The report then went on to ask if the present system of signalling was adequate and if a driver could do all his duties while still looking out for signals when there could often be several signals passed within a few minutes.

In-cab signalling was a system in use on some railways in Britain. It was seen as a much safer system. *The Guardian* described it as popular with engineers but unpopular with the directors of railway companies due to the expense.

The last serious accident to occur before the outbreak of the First World War happened on 17 June 1914. It was different to other rail accidents in that some of the fatalities drowned.

The accident happened on the Highland Railway near Carrbridge and involved the train from Perth to Inverness. The tender came off the line, taking a passenger carriage with it, which fell into a stream. Due to heavy rain the stream was very high. Three of the passengers were swept out of the carriage and were drowned. News of the accident was hard to get due to telegram and telephone communication problems. On 19 June, however, *The Times* managed to print a story relating to the accident.

According to *The Times*'s story the engine became detached from the train on a culvert. The tender was derailed and then the culvert collapsed. Three bodies were found in the river but it was not known how many were washed away. A sailor from HMS *Amphion* helped rescue those in trouble.

The Manchester Guardian report went into more detail about the result of the accident on the carriage. The stream that the carriage fell into was a tributary of the river Dulnain. The shock of the fall and the rush of water burst open the doors of the carriage. It also ripped off the roof. It was not known how many passengers were in the carriage at the time of the accident.

CHAPTER 11

The First World War

The outbreak of the war led to some drastic changes in the railway system in Britain. Trains were the most useful way of moving goods for the war effort as well as men from one place to another. Although the previous few years had been relatively peaceful with regard to the number of accidents and fatalities on the railways, this was to change. The year 1915 was to be the worst year for a decade for the number of fatal crashes but was also to be the worst year ever for the number of fatalities, including the highest number of deaths in a single railway accident ever to occur in Britain.

It wasn't very long into the war before the first fatal accident occurred. It happened on 1 January 1915 on the Great Eastern Railway at Ilford. Ten people died when two trains collided near the station.

According to *The Times,* a local train left Gidea Park at 8.20 am for Liverpool Street. It was full of passengers from the suburbs of Ilford, Goodmayes and Seven Kings who were on their way to London. It passed through Ilford without stopping and moved across the fast line to London just as the Clacton express, also going to London, arrived on the line it was crossing.

The collision cut the train in half as it hit two First Class carriages. Both were completely wrecked and the carriages behind them all overturned. The engine of the express went off the line into a coal yard behind a paper mill and killed a horse. All the dead were from the local train; they included two workers from the GER. There were also a number of GER employees among the injured. It seems many of those employed in the railway offices at Liverpool Street lived in Goodmayes. It was believed that the signals were set for the local train.

The Guardian of 2 July said that the slow Gidea Park train normally followed the Clacton train, which was supposed to have the right of way. It was stated that the signals had been for the slow train but then, according to the report, someone else claimed that the express had the right of way.

A small crowd has gathered to look at this overturned engine. Unfortunately, there are no details of where this accident took place.

The waiting passengers on the platform at Ilford witnessed the accident and quickly went to help the injured. Local residents also came to help. There was an eyewitness statement from George Mills, the landlord of the nearby White Horse public house. He said that arms were sticking through the wheels of the train while the rest of the bodies could not be seen. Also helping were soldiers, civil guards and police. *The Guardian* mentioned brave rescue work by soldiers and the police but did not mention the civilians. The soldiers were territorials who were guarding the line and others employed elsewhere near the station.

The one woman who died was in an undamaged part of the train. According to *The Times*'s report, she was still sitting bolt upright and had died of shock. A man who had both legs cut off was carried away from the wreckage. He said, 'Thanks old chap,' and died. Notices listing the names of the injured and which hospital they had been taken to were put up in shop windows near the station for the benefit of relatives searching for loved ones.

Britain's worst ever railway disaster occurred during the war, on 22 May 1915, and involved a troop train in which a large number of soldiers died.

Three trains collided at Quintinshill, an isolated signal box about 10 miles from Carlisle, and then caught fire. The accident illustrated the danger of wooden trains that were lit by gas, although this was already common knowledge due to previous instances. *The Times* reported that 'it may be recalled that in eight out of thirteen accidents in recent years in which the wreckage caught fire it was due to an escape of gas.'

The trains involved were the express for Edinburgh from Euston, which was supposed to leave at 11.45 pm but was running about an hour late. It was made up of two trains that would later separate for different destinations. Also involved was the local Caledonian Railway passenger train.

The accident was caused by the actions of two signalmen, George Meakin and James Tinsley. The two men had an arrangement where the man on night duty would stay a bit later so the day man could delay his arrival. This also meant that the man going to work could get a ride on one of the local trains.

The troops involved in the accident were territorials. Although they would normally be used for home defence during the war many were being sent abroad, and this was what was happening with the 1/7 Royal Scots. The men

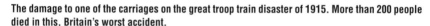

The damage to one of the carriages on the great troop train disaster of 1915. More than 200 people died in this, Britain's worst accident.

Another view of the troop train disaster, showing the burnt remains of a sleeping car. There were some rumours that men were trapped behind locked doors.

were packed in, eight to a compartment. It was later reported that many of the compartment doors may have been locked.

The first train to arrive on the scene was a goods train. What to do with trains was the responsibility of the signalman. Meakin was on duty and put the goods train into the down loop until the two express trains passed. Then an empty coal train arrived that had delivered its load to the fleet at Scapa Flow. Meakin planned to put this on the up loop while he dealt with the local train, which arrived with Tinsley on board, as he had got a lift. Tinsley put the local train on the up line, which was unusual. He then put the coal train on the up loop.

The Times published a statement from James Tinsley. He said he had been at Quintinshill for five years. As both sidings were full he had put the local train onto the up line while the express passed. He said he had no alternative and that this was done regularly. It had been there for fifteen minutes before the troop train hit it.

It was the local passenger train that was hit by the troop train. Then the wreckage was hit by the Scottish express from Euston. There were four lines at this point, two being sidings, and five trains. The local train was moved to one line to let the express pass and was then hit by the troop train. The troop train was carrying about 500 men and officers and was going south.

There were various reports on the number of casualties. *The Observer* of 23 May said that more than seventy soldiers had been killed and 300 injured. They also said that some of the soldiers had been to the front and had seen nothing so horrible in the trenches. According to *The Times* on 24 May, the total number of dead was 158, but the number could reach 170 as there were so many injured. The final death toll was 226 – much worse than early reports had suggested. Many of the dead were burnt to death and were unrecognizable. *The Times*'s report said the victims were helpless through injury or trapped by wreckage but there were also rumours of carriage doors being locked. *The Guardian* of the same day said there were 200 dead and also published photographs of the wreckage.

Among the first witnesses on the scene, according to *The Times,* were the couple who acted as caretakers of the nearby marrying blacksmiths shop at Gretna Green. Mrs Dunbar said that the crash was so tremendous that she thought the Germans had invaded. The men trapped in the carriages were calling for help as the fire spread. Some of those who had escaped then began to force open the doors.

The roll call of troops after the disaster. There were fifty-two out of 500, but many of the uninjured had accompanied the wounded to hospital.

Although the vast majority of the dead were soldiers from the troop train there were also some deaths in the sleeping saloon of the express train. The driver and fireman of the troop train also died but it seems there were no fatalities on the local train.

The Times printed a list of the previous twelve worst rail accidents in Britain. As well as describing the accident the newspaper published two other articles on the same day; one included a soldier's dying words: 'If only it was a fight.' There were a number of connections with the war in the report such as they 'fought through the wreckage as though storming a German trench.' Most of the men had apparently been asleep when the accident happened.

By 25 May *The Guardian* had a list of those who had died. This included 199 soldiers, the driver and fireman of the troop train and eleven passengers in the express. By the following day they were considering what had happened to cause the accident. *The Guardian* had previously assumed that the signalman had not known about the troop train because he hadn't been told or he had forgotten about it. They then published a statement from Tinsley

The engine tender of the express that ran into the troop train. The accident was due to the signalmen forgetting where they parked a train.

saying that he had been told about the troop train and where the local train was but had forgotten where the local train had been put.

The use of trains for moving troops had previously been uneventful. There were 350 trains carrying troops to Southampton in forty-eight hours to carry the Expeditionary Force. Seventy trains a day were unloaded at the port after this and several thousand troop trains had since run with no accidents.

The Board of Trade report written by Lieutenant Colonel E. Druitt put the blame for the accident squarely on the shoulders of the two signalmen for their neglect of the rules. As well as their breach of the rules it seems that Meakin was still in the signal box after his shift had finished and was reading a newspaper, making others in the signal box aware of news stories in it and distracting them from their duty.

More details were included in the report such as the fact that many of the soldiers who had escaped the collision were then run down by the express as it crashed into the wreckage. Druitt also claimed that the fire would have started even if the carriages had not been lit by gas. This would have been due to the ash from the engines.

The next serious accident of the year occurred in August. Ten people died on an Irish express from Euston to Holyhead on the 14th of the month. The train went off the rails between Stowe Tunnel and Weedon Station in Northamptonshire. Seven of the carriages then rolled down an embankment.

The train had just passed the express from Rugby to London when the accident occurred. The first two coaches were Post Office sorting vans. The next was partly a guard's van and a Third Class carriage. Most of the deaths occurred in the fifth and sixth carriages, which telescoped.

The cause was, according to *The Times*'s report, the steel rod connecting the wheels of the passing Rugby train breaking and striking the front engine of the Holyhead train as they passed. The driver of the Holyhead engine said he saw something fly off the Rugby engine. It was claimed by a Rugby official, however, that although the rod had broken, it had not become detached. Another theory was that the broken rod may have damaged the line.

There was a statement in *The Times* by a soldier who had been on the train. Private James Doherty DCM had fought at Ypres and was on his way home to Waterford. His carriage ended up on its side. Along with some other soldiers, he helped get the injured out while also stopping to help a lady collect £50 in gold that had been scattered around her compartment.

Another man, Joseph Milland of Dublin, stepped out into the corridor to smoke just before the accident occurred, leaving his daughter of eighteen in the compartment. When the accident happened the carriage turned over but

Express Engines Wrecked,
Gretna Green Railway Disaster May 22. 1915

The engine of the express involved in the troop train crash. There are a number of different postcards of the accident.

landed with the corridor upwards. Milland was unhurt but later found his daughter dying in a local hospital.

The Observer of 15 August was more concerned with the notable people who had been on the train. Lord Monteagle and Colonel Lynch MP had been injured. An ex-MP, Sir Lees Knowles and his new wife, escaped unhurt. *The Guardian* of the following day had an interesting comment in that the train had been spared fire, 'which had been the worst torment in recent railway accidents.' This was supposedly due to the carriages being lit by electricity instead of gas.

The final serious accident of the year occurred just before Christmas on 17 December at St Bedes Junction near South Shields, on the North Eastern Railway. There were nineteen deaths and a large number of injuries. Once again, fire was a major factor in the accident.

The accident involved the 7.05 am train from South Shields, which was used by businessmen and workmen. It was seven coaches long and was busy, having picked up a large number of passengers for Sunderland at Tyne Dock, mainly from the naval yards. The train hit a light engine that was on the same line. Then an empty passenger train from Jarrow came into collision with the wreckage.

The first carriages of the packed train were the worst damaged. These then caught fire, stopping those passengers who hadn't been injured from getting any of the injured out. The first three coaches were damaged, the middle one of the three being completely destroyed. The engine had been assisting a heavy goods train from Tyne Dock and left the train at St Bedes Junction. It was standing on the main line waiting to go back into the dock when the passenger train came along and hit it.

The Times published a witness account from a passenger. Munitions worker John Eales found himself in pitch darkness and unable to move after the accident. The compartment then filled with gas and one end burst into flame. Passengers at the other end of the carriage were screaming. He suddenly found himself free from the wreckage and managed to get out.

The Guardian of the 15th claimed that most of those killed had been munitions workers. They went on to argue that they had died in their country's service as truly as soldiers at the front. In most cases they had in

Another view of an accident that has no details of the place or time of the event.

their last moments had to suffer a more terrible time than what soldiers had to endure. The writer obviously considered that being shot or blown up was a better death than one by fire. The report went on to ask when railway carriages' gas lighting, which caused so many problems, would be abolished in favour of electricity.

After the terrible year of 1915 there were no serious accidents on the railways in the following year. This was not to last into 1917 and on 3 January twelve people were killed in an accident near Edinburgh. It was a similar accident to the last one there in December 1915 in that the 4.18 pm express from Edinburgh to Glasgow hit a light engine that was on the same line. There was some doubt as to how many had died and *The Guardian* of 4 January reported that they didn't know how many had died. It wasn't until the next day they reported that there had been twelve deaths.

When the accident occurred at Ratho Station the train was very busy with workers, soldiers and sailors all returning home from the New Year's holiday. The weather was stormy and the site of the accident was desolate. The first coach of the express was telescoped into the second.

The Times printed an interesting interview with a survivor who said that when the collision took place the lights went out, the windows broke and the doors jammed. This was interesting because in other accidents there had been some doubt as to whether doors were locked or had become jammed as a result of the accident. The military men then squeezed out of the windows to run and help those trapped.

The servicemen who had been on the trains were directed by some officers who had also been passengers. They were doing such a good job that the civilians were happy to stand and watch and let them get on with it.

There were no more serious crashes in 1917 but there was a serious train-related accident on 24 September at Bere Ferrers, near Plymouth. A train carrying New Zealand troops had stopped at the station. A number of the men got out on the wrong side and were on the tracks as an express train came along and hit them, killing ten. It seems that accidents such as these were not as notable as train crashes. *The Guardian* of 25 September had only a short stop press article saying that nine New Zealanders had been killed.

The final serious accident of the war period took place on 19 January 1918. It happened on the Midland Railway at Little Salkeld, 15 miles south of Carlisle. It involved another Scottish express train from London to Glasgow. The train ran into part of the cutting, which had collapsed onto the line. The collision resulted in seven deaths.

The Times's report mentioned that the site of the accident was only a few

The derailed engine and damaged coaches of the accident at Little Salkeld in 1918. The train hit a collapsed embankment.

Cranes in place to lift the wreckage at Little Salkeld. The remote position has deterred large crowds of spectators.

miles from Hawes Junction, where twelve people had died in an accident in December 1910, as well as Aisgill, where fourteen died in September 1913, and Quintinshill, where 226 people died in May 1915. *The Guardian* also mentioned previous accidents in the area.

The driver of the train had seen the earth begin to slide from the cutting as he approached it. He applied the brake but could not stop in time. The engine mounted the pile of earth, stopping the train, which caused the first carriage to be telescoped into the tender. All the casualties were in the first two coaches.

In all the accidents that occurred during the First World War there were soldiers on the trains involved. This one was no exception and it was the military men who were to do most of the work releasing those trapped in the wreckage. When the relief train arrived it took some of the injured to the Fusehill military hospital at Carlisle. These were injured soldiers.

One of these, Lieutenant Thompson RFC, said in *The Guardian* of 21 December that he saw passengers' legs protruding from the wreckage. Among the dead were three boys and three women. However, Mr Thomas, the assistant inspector of the Midland Railway, who was on the train, was unhurt.

CHAPTER 12

1918 to 1939

The end of the war was to see a break of three years before another serious rail accident occurred. This one was at Abermule on the Cambrian Railway in Wales, on 26 January 1921. There was a head-on collision on a single line system between an express and a local train, which resulted in seventeen deaths.

There was much made of the tablet system in *The Times*'s report. This was a means of controlling the trains where a driver would be given a tablet at a station. This would then automatically lock the repository of the tablet at the next station. Once the driver of the express train was given the tablet it would have been impossible for the local train driver to have got the tablet at the next station, but this was what happened.

There seems to have been a serious attempt at investigative journalism in *The Times* as the writer of the story went to Abermule Station to find out what had happened, but found that the staff had changed. A railway official said it was up to the fireman to make sure he had the correct tablet.

An inquiry was held under Lieutenant Colonel J.W. Pringle, chief inspecting officer of the Ministry of Transport. Pringle had held a Board of Trade investigation into a similar accident on the Cambrian Railway three years earlier, when two goods trains had collided. It seems that in that case two tablets for the same section were out at the same time.

The Guardian report of 1 March mentioned that the inquiry could not be completed as some passengers were still in hospital. The Cambrian Railway officials had claimed that all measures to guard against a reoccurrence of the accident had been carried out. They argued that only one other accident on a single line had occurred since the tablet system had been introduced thirty years before.

Pringle's inquiry found that the driver of the slow local train involved in the accident had been given a tablet that was not applicable to that section of the line. There had been irregular practice among the staff at the station at

Abermule and there was a relief stationmaster there when the accident happened. It is also interesting to note that the lighting in the carriages of both trains was a mixture of gas and electric.

The problems faced by railway companies after an accident did not end with clearing the track. *The Guardian* of 21 February 1922 reported that John Reed, who had been a passenger on the train that crashed, had been awarded £1,500 damages at Salop Assizes. He had suffered no broken limbs in the accident but had been a nervous wreck ever since. The Cambrian Railway did not accept the court rulings easily and in the case of another victim of the accident, Reginald Davies, at Chester, they contested his injuries. Davies was claiming £384 due to damage to his big toe, which meant he could not walk very far.

It looked as though safety was improving as there was another three-year gap before the next serious accident. This was an unusual one in that the 4.40 pm train from Liverpool to Lytham and Blackpool on the London Midland

A fallen engine at Waterside in 1929.

and Scottish Railway was derailed and hit a signal box near Lytham. The box fell over and caught fire.

The *Times*'s report of 4 November stated that five bodies had been recovered and taken to Lytham Station. It went on to say that seven or eight others may have died. *The Guardian* of the same day said that there had been ten bodies recovered and there were three still under the wreckage. The situation was described as a midnight search for the dead. Eventually it was found that fourteen people had died.

The engine had come off the line about 100 yards before the signal box. The first two carriages came off the line and turned over. The next stayed on the line, but the next two turned over and caught fire. The signalman was thrown out of the wreckage, over a fence and into a brook. He had minor injuries. Passengers stopped another train before it could hit the wreckage.

On realizing that the train had left the rails, a number of passengers had decided to jump out. Unfortunately, they chose the wrong side of the train and the carriage fell on to them. The accident, according to *The Times*, was due to the fracture of a tyre on the engine. *The Guardian* thought it had either jumped the points or an axle had broken.

A more unusual accident took place on 30 August 1926 when the 1.18 pm express train from Newcastle hit a charabanc on a level crossing at Naworth, near Carlisle. The nine dead were mainly passengers on the charabanc, although one of the victims was the porter who opened the gate to allow the charabanc to cross. He had only been working there a week and did not know the job well. *The Guardian* concentrated on the danger of travel by charabanc. The vehicles had claimed many victims in the past and there had been three fatal charabanc accidents in 1925.

The Ministry of Transport report on the accident was written by Lieutenant Colonel A.H.L. Mount. He found that the porter who had been in charge of the crossing gates on the day of the accident was a war veteran who had passed an exam on the use of the level crossing gates. The normal weekly traffic across the crossing was about fifty motor vehicles, twelve carts and thirty-six bicycles and prams. Before opening the gates the person in charge was supposed to check the position of trains on the line. For some reason on that day the porter did not do this but just opened the gates as the charabanc approached the crossing. It was impossible to find out why this was, because he was killed as well.

The next accident occurred on 19 November 1926, on the London, Midland and Scottish Railway, with the York to Bristol express. It came off the rails after hitting a goods train as it passed between Rawmarsh and

Staff safety had become an issue on the railways and a prevention of accidents book was issued. The introduction of electric rails was an obvious danger to those used to walking on the lines.

Masborough stations and nine people died. Many of the deaths were caused by part of the goods wagons penetrating the passenger coaches and hitting passengers sitting on that side of the train. According to *The Times*, this was caused by doors breaking open on the goods trains and some of the items inside protruding into the passing train.

The Guardian concentrated their report on how the sides had been ripped off the passenger carriages. The report said that 'the sides were ripped off as though they were the cover of a book.' *The Guardian* then went on to complain how the carriages had been shunted into sidings by a high street so that anyone could see them. It also mentioned that thousands had come to look, which means that they must have mostly been sightseers.

After a few years without any serious accidents there were two in 1926 and again in 1927. The first of 1927 was at Hull Paragon on 14 February on the London and North Eastern Railway, when there was a collision between two trains resulting in twelve deaths.

The Times of 15 February asked why the outgoing train to Scarborough leaving Paragon Station at 9.05 am should have run into the incoming train from Withernsea. Why were the trains, which were going in opposite directions, travelling on the same line?

There was damage to both trains, with the first coach of the

Scarborough train telescoping into the tender and the first coach of the Withernsea train mounting the tender and engine. A number of the dead were children on their way to school. A nearby Poor Law institution had a hole knocked in the wall so the injured could be passed through straight into the building.

The Guardian also mentioned that the train was full of children on their way to school, along with teachers and businessmen. They explained how doctors and nurses had to climb over the wall of the Poor Law institution but they called it a naval hospital. Then a breach was made in the wall to allow access for the injured.

Although many of the injured were thrown out onto the line as the carriages burst there were also a number of passengers trapped. Many of these were children. A doctor's dresser who was involved in the rescue work said that what struck him most were the demeanours of the children, who were neither crying or groaning but were cheerful and brave. There was no explanation as to the cause of the accident.

The second accident of the year occurred on the Southern Railway on 24 August near Sevenoaks. It involved the 5.00 pm express from Cannon Street to Deal. There were thirteen deaths and a number of injured. As the train approached a bridge at Riverhead it had begun to sway. This was due to subsidence because of recent heavy rain. The train came off the tracks as it passed under the bridge. The engine and the first few coaches cleared the bridge but the third coach hit the bridge and was smashed to pieces.

The Guardian report revealed how the chances of being hurt were down to the choice of carriage. The first carriage was destroyed, as was the third. The second was still intact and was used as offices for officials of the Southern Rail Company.

It was interesting that alongside the report on the accident was a story about telephone wires being cut and stolen on the London and North Eastern Railway. It seems that the culprits were stealing copper wire, which has been an offence much in the news recently but obviously dates back a long way.

The engine went on before toppling over against the bank near Sevenoaks Station. Motor cars rushed from all parts of the district, according to *The Times*. The availability of these cars made it possible to get the injured to hospital quickly.

The following year, 1928, was to see an increase in the number of serious accidents and was the worst for some time, despite the first accident not occurring until June. The Doncaster accident, a head-on collision, occurred on 27 June and led to twenty-five deaths, the highest toll since 1915.

Some of the photographs in the accident prevention book seem to show obvious ways of staying safe, such as this one showing it was not safe to walk with your back to the direction of traffic.

One of the trains was an excursion train from Newcastle to Scarborough and back. Due to the holiday nature of the train fourteen of the dead came from the same small town, Hetton-le-Hole in County Durham. They were part of a Mother's Union outing.

A spokesman from the London and North Eastern Railway said that the excursion was on its way back from Scarborough and as it passed Darlington Top Bank Station at 11.20 pm it collided with an engine of a parcel train that was shunting vehicles. The engine of the excursion train turned over and three carriages were wrecked.

In the report in *The Guardian* the headline claimed that the train had only been travelling at 10 miles per hour. Carriages telescoped and one body was thrown onto the roof of one of these. One must wonder how many would have died if the train had been travelling at a faster speed. The newspaper also recorded a list of recent rail accidents.

There was no explanation as to the cause of the accident. Both drivers seemed to think that they had the right of way. There seemed to be less chance of the newspaper reports publishing the cause based on rumour or unfounded views than there had been in the past.

The next serious accident to occur in 1927 was at London Bridge on 9 July. There were two deaths, although *The Times* of 10 July only reported one. The train involved was an electric train from London Bridge to Epsom, which hit a light engine. The train was of the Southern Railway Company and the accident was the first to have occurred since many of the local lines had been converted to electricity the previous March.

Based on passenger statements and the position of the train, the train and engine were moving in the same direction on separate lines. The lines then converged about 100 yards from the station. It was at this point that the engine hit the second coach of the train.

Once again, *The Guardian* had a report that concentrated on the speed of the trains involved. It claimed that the engine was only travelling at 2 or 3 miles an hour and the train itself was only travelling at 15 miles an hour. As the accident occurred on an electric line the current had to be cut off before any rescue could take place.

A passenger, Mr Lowe, gave his version of what happened in *The Times*. He suffered a broken nose and was alone in a compartment in the second carriage. There was a loud crash and the carriage fell to pieces around him. He remained conscious and was trapped until someone released him.

The next serious accident of the year took place on 13 October at Charfield in Gloucestershire and led to fifteen deaths. A statement from the London,

Midland and Scottish Railway in *The Times,* of 15 October stated that the 10.00 pm mail train from Leeds to Bristol ran into a shunting freight train in thick fog. The report said that only two had died but there may have been more in the wreckage.

According to *The Times,* many of the injured may have been saved had it not been for the fact that the mail train caught fire due to the gas lighting in the carriages and this was what led to many of the deaths. In the words of the report, they 'had to be abandoned and died in the flames.'

The Guardian had more information on this on 14 October, when it said that the Bath train had burst into flames, but this was not only due to the gas but also to petrol tanks on the goods train. The report went on to say that there had already been fifty deaths in rail accidents in 1928.

Another seemingly obvious thing not to do: look before stepping from behind a train. When the author trained as a guard in the 1970s, he was shown photographs of the results of some workers who did not do the obvious.

The engine of the mail train just caught the freight train as it was clearing the main line. The carriages behind the engine telescoped and climbed above the engine and hit a bridge. Many of the passengers were trapped by the legs as the seats were forced together. One woman told how the fire was getting nearer and she shielded herself with a travel rug until released.

The Times's reporter examined the bridge where the carriages had burned. He said that the road surface had melted due to the heat and run to the sides of the bridge. The bridge had been closed to traffic since the accident.

There were to be another two serious accidents in 1929 but the number of fatalities was lower than in the previous accidents. The first was on 8 January at Ashchurch Station, near Cheltenham. It involved the Bristol to Birmingham mail train, which left Cheltenham at 8.40 pm, and there were four deaths.

The train had just passed through Ashchurch Station when it ran into a goods train that was being shunted. The engine and two coaches were wrecked and others were derailed. There was thick fog, which along with the darkness made rescue very difficult. The gas lights in one of the carriages were still alight but there was no fire. *The Guardian* of 9 January described how the rescue work was carried on by the light of a large bonfire of wreckage from the crash. There were still bodies underneath the wreck but the rescuers had to wait for cranes to release them.

Despite the accident occurring late in the evening, about 9.00 pm, *The Times*'s report stated that news of the accident spread quickly and large numbers of people came to help. The London Midland and Scottish Railway made a statement saying that the driver of the mail train had died and four people were injured. Official statements usually seemed to underestimate the numbers of dead and injured.

The accident that occurred on 20 November on the Somerset and Dorset Railway was unusual in that all of the three fatalities were railway employees. This was because the accident involved a coal train so had no passengers on board. The train ran away on a steep incline from the Coombe Down Tunnel. It eventually crashed into buildings at a goods yard at Bath. One man was found dead on the line and two others in the wreckage.

The Guardian headline of 21 November said: 'Runaway goods train dash into shed'. The report explained that one of the dead who had been on the train was Inspector Norman, who was in charge of the goods yard where the train crashed.

For the next few years there seemed to be a lull in the seriousness of accidents. Those accidents that did occur had low numbers of fatalities. On 22 March 1931 there was a derailment at Leighton Buzzard. The accident involved the Scottish express from Euston, the first fatal accident for some time.

The Guardian of 23 March described the train as a 'famous express derailed'. This was the *Royal Scot*, which when it came off the rails was, according to a railway official, travelling at 30 miles per hour. It was tearing up the track, throwing sleepers right and left.

The London, Midland and Scottish train had left London at 11.30 am. It reached Leighton Buzzard Station at 12.15, when it left the rails and crashed. This resulted in six deaths, including Sir George Saltmarsh, a former member of the Port of London Authority.

The train had been travelling on the fast down line but there were repairs being made to the line beyond the station. Because of this the train had to change over to the slow line. It was where the train crossed onto the other line that it came off the rails. The first four coaches were destroyed.

A woman and her daughter were trapped from the waist down beneath one of the carriages. They were eventually freed using a steam crane to raise the carriage but had been in their position for four hours. The Scottish

Clearing up after an accident at Northallerton. (www.transporttreasury.co.uk)

national football team, which had played England at Stamford Bridge the previous day, were also on the train, but were uninjured.

The Ministry of Transport report was written by Lieutenant Colonel A.H.L. Mount. He found that there had been a failure by the driver to obey the signals. Both the driver and the fireman were killed, so it was impossible to question them. It was also found that special notices about the diversions were not seen by the guard on the train.

There was a change in the reporting of railway crashes after the First World War in that rail companies were quick to make a statement about accidents. In the nineteenth century there were often complaints by newspapers that rail companies were reluctant to give any information after an accident.

When an accident happened on 25 May 1933 at Raynes Park, the Southern Railway made a statement that was published in *The Times* the next day. It announced that a steam train that left Waterloo at 3.10 pm to Alton became derailed between Wimbledon and Raynes Park and hit another train approaching on the up line. The report admitted that five people had died.

All the deaths were on the Waterloo train, although the driver of the other train did break his arm. Included in the deaths was a child of a family from America. The Duties family from Portland Oregon were British and had returned from America on business and to visit friends. One of their children died and the other was injured.

The Guardian headline of 26 May described it as 'a strange London disaster'. The Alton train had left the line and hit the Southampton train side-on. The newspaper also described the incident as the worst railway accident for two years.

The Times's report mentioned a Mrs Hitchcock, who had an accident in her car at Hayward's Heath, where her vehicle collided with a lorry. She phoned home to tell her family of her narrow escape and was told that her husband had died in the train crash.

The Times's report did not go into detail about why the accident happened but did publish a short biography of each of those who died on the train.

The year 1934 saw a rise in the number of deaths in rail accidents. There were two fatal accidents in the month of September, the first at Port Eglinton Junction at Glasgow.

There was also a head-on collision in which nine people died on the London Midland and Scottish Railway. The trains involved were a passenger train from Kilmarnock and a suburban train from Paisley to Glasgow. *The Times*'s report of 7 September only gave the number of dead as two. One fatality was a driver and the other a passenger. According to *The Guardian* the engine driver was trapped against the firebox and was burned to death. Many of the injured were thrown out of the train and were found unconscious on the line.

The engine of the Paisley train hit one of the coaches of the other train. Carriages on both trains were badly damaged. There was no explanation in *The Times*'s report as to why the accident happened.

Later the same month another accident occurred on the London Midland and Scottish Railway at Winwick, near Warrington. Twelve people died in a collision. The 5.20 express from Euston to Blackpool on 28 September ran into the rear of another train, the Warrington to Earlsestown, just past Winwick Junction. The engine of the express smashed the rear carriage of the local train.

The Guardian of 29 September said that reliable sources reported that eight had died: five men and three women. A reporter at Newton-le-Willows hospital had informed the newspaper that ten or twelve had died. The report went on to say that someone had telephoned Warrington Infirmary at midnight and was told that twenty-one passengers had been admitted with injuries but there had been no fatalities.

There was a strange report in *The Times* about the driver of the express, named Steel, who was said by some to have been helping with the rescue of those trapped. Other reports said that he was dead or missing. Almost all the injuries and deaths were on the express but the driver of the slow train hurt his arm. The engine of this train was at the back.

The slow train had left Warrington at 8.55 and stopped at Winswick Junction. The express then passed through Warrington at 8.59, just four minutes behind the slow train. This seems very close together.

The following year there was an accident on 15 June at Welwyn Garden City. There were thirteen deaths and more than eighty injured. It was a collision on the London and North Eastern Railway involving the 10.45 pm express from King's Cross to Newcastle. It stopped at a signal and the 10.50 parcel train from King's Cross to York ran into the back of it.

The Guardian printed a statement from a railway official saying that the King's Cross to Newcastle was in duplicate, which meant that two trains instead of one were sent. It was the second of these that was run into by the parcel train.

Although the last few coaches of the first train were damaged the greater damage was to the carriages on the second train. *The Times* described this as a 'dog and monkey train' – one that took all kinds of cargo such as horseboxes, fish vans and parcel trucks as well as passengers. There were forty passengers in the second train and all were either injured or killed.

Clearing up after what was obviously a serious accident. Unfortunately, there are no details of where this accident was.

The chief mechanical engineer of the company, Mr H. Gresley, arrived at the site and was surprised how few casualties there were on the first train. After examining the wreckage he claimed that this was due to the strength of the new rolling stock on the Newcastle train. It would seem that new carriages did not burst to atoms in a collision as many of the old carriages had done in previous accidents.

Although the Newcastle train was fitted with a Buck Eye or Gould coupling, which locks the carriage frames together, the three least damaged carriages on the second train also had these couplings, indicating that the modern equipment was much safer than the old stock. The front of the express was able to carry on with its journey after the accident.

There were a number of dead passengers who had not been identified and *The Times* published descriptions of them. These included a woman aged thirty-five to forty with stout build and no teeth and a woman of about fifty-one with two prominent front teeth.

The following year, 1936, was a good one; there was only one serious accident, with only two fatalities. This was at Shrivenham on the Great Western Railway. It involved a collision between an express train and some goods trucks. The express was the 9.00 pm mail and boat train from Penzance to Paddington. It was travelling at about 60 miles an hour when it ran into some trucks that had broken free from a coal train. The guard from the goods train had tried to stop the express but it was too late.

There was a noticeable difference in the extent of damage to the carriages than in the last crash. The first two coaches of the express, which were of wood, were smashed. The third carriage was of metal, so was probably more modern. This one was undamaged. The engine of the express was also badly damaged and the driver later died in hospital.

Photographs of the wreckage appeared in *The Guardian*. The story accompanying these said that a bonfire had been built out of the wreckage to warm the injured. They had been laid on cushions from the train round the fire. It was also claimed that before this accident only one person had died accidently on the GWR in the past twenty years.

There was a collision between two electric trains on 2 April 1937 on the Southern Railway near Battersea Park Station. Ten people died. It happened at eight o'clock in the morning. *The Times* said that it was the first fatal railway accident in inner London since 1924.

The trains involved were the 7.31 am train from Coulsdon North to Victoria, which ran into the back of the 7.30 train from London Bridge to Victoria. The first train was stopped on a viaduct, which, according to *The Times*, was 30 feet high. The collision caused a flash, which was thought to be a fire, but it was a short circuit that caused the power to switch off.

The rear coach of the first train and the front coach of the rear train were the most severely damaged. Where recent accidents had led to less serious results when they involved new carriages, this one was the opposite. *The Times* report mentioned that the age of the carriages was an advantage in that they were old. Because they were partly wood, they stayed on the viaduct. If they had been modern steel carriages then the weight would have taken them off the viaduct onto the street 30 feet below.

It was interesting that *The Guardian* claimed that the viaduct was 60 feet high, twice the height stated in *The Times*'s report. They also published lots of photographs and explained how glass and wood were showered on the yard of A. Hunter & Sons, organ builders, which was below the site of the accident.

The Ministry of Transport report was written by Lieutenant Colonel A.H.L. Mount. He found that there was a relief signalman in charge of the Battersea Park Junction signal box. He did not seem to be able to deal with things as they went wrong and he had become confused.

There were also some comments on the construction of carriages. The two rear carriages on the first train had telescoped and this was where many fatalities took place. Mount said if they had been of stronger construction this may not have happened. He also said that shock-absorbing buffers would help cut down on damage in a collision.

The worst railway accident to happen for more than twenty years took place on 10 December 1937 on the London and North Eastern Railway. Thirty-five people died at Castlecary, near Falkirk, in a severe snowstorm when an express train from Glasgow to Edinburgh ran into a stationary train from Dundee to Glasgow at 4.45 pm. *The Times*'s report of 11 December gave the number of dead as twenty-four.

The Guardian of the same day said that they didn't know the exact number of dead but it was the worst accident since 1915. They described it as a collision in a blizzard. There was a foot of snow on the ground and snow was still falling after the accident. A nearby goods shed was being used as a mortuary.

The snow hampered the rescue attempts and the number of fatalities was still unknown at the time of the report in *The Times* on 11 December. The Dundee train was stopped at a signal when the express ran into the back of it. The pure chance of the railway accident was shown by the express driver being thrown clear and surviving while the fireman was killed instantly.

A passenger in the second compartment of the express survived with few injuries, as did others in his compartment. However, the carriage behind this was telescoped and the passenger said that it was in this carriage that most of the deaths occurred. The rear carriages were undamaged and passengers in these were unaware how serious the crash had been.

CHAPTER 13

The Second World War

T he strain placed on British railways during the Second World War was even greater than that in the previous war. There was much more danger from enemy air raids and people also had to deal with the blackout. This was not only difficult for passengers who would arrive at dark stations with no signs, it was also challenging for drivers approaching darkened platforms.

There was a serious accident on 4 November 1940 at Norton Fitzwarren, near Taunton, on the Great Western Railway. The 9.50 pm express from Paddingtion to Penzance was derailed and twenty-seven people died. Many had been asleep due to the late timing of the train.

The train was crowded with passengers, many of them servicemen. The engine came off the line and the first four carriages were telescoped. *The Times* of 5 November listed twenty-four dead, which was the number known at the time. There were a number of sailors amongst the dead as well as a woman and her two children.

A railway official of the GWR said that the cause could not be found until the wreckage was cleared. He was certain that it was an accident and confirmed it was not due to enemy action or sabotage.

The accident happened at 4.00 am. The driver survived and managed to run to the nearby station and had the signal put at danger to stop any more trains coming. A sailor who survived thought that the train had been bombed. One passenger thought he saw aircraft wings but it turned out to be pieces of coach debris standing at angles.

The reason for the crash became clear after the Ministry of War Transport investigation under Lieutenant Colonel A.H.L. Mount. The results were reported in *The Manchester Guardian* on 28 December 1940. It was due to an

An accident at Church Fenton in 1943. The image is from an old photographic glass plate.

unaccountable lapse by P.W. Stacey, a driver with forty years' experience on the GWR. The sole cause of the disaster was that Stacey was watching for signals on the main line but was actually driving on the relief line. It was thought this may have been due to the blackout.

The first serious accidents of the war were confined to trains to or from the West Country and occurred on the Great Western Railway. There was another fatal crash on 2 July 1941 at Dolphin Junction, near Slough. Five people died when a passenger train from Plymouth had a head-on collision with a goods train. Again it happened during the night, at 3.00 am.

Due to the war many of the passengers on trains were members of the services and three of the dead in this accident were naval men. *The Times* mentioned that the majority of the passengers were servicemen on their way to London on leave. The accident occurred on the crossover point from the main up line to the slow line.

Much of the rescue work was carried out by servicemen, including some of those who had been on the train, with help from the ARP and other civil defence men from Slough. Help was also give by some Home Guard units who were in the area.

As with other reports on railway accidents at this time, there was no mention of what had caused the accident in the early *Times* report. There seemed to be less of a will to publish rumours as to what happened as there had been in the past. A later *Times* report on 14 July said that the GWR accepted liability for the accident but still gave no reason for why it happened.

It wasn't until 5 November 1941 when a further report appeared in *The Times* that said it was the signalman who was blamed for the accident. Major G. Wilson in his report to the Ministry of War Transport said that the signalman, Welch, had claimed he had made a mistake in assuming that the goods train had stopped. There was no reason why Welch didn't divert the goods train onto the up relief so the express could pass.

The Guardian of the same date also reported on the reasons for the accident. They mentioned how the driver of the goods train was surprised to see the home signal at danger at a range of 300 to 400 yards. According to the newspaper, Major Wilson commented that the signalman's statement saying he thought the goods train had come to a stop was clearly false.

The accident that occurred on 30 December 1941 was different from the last two in that there was no mention of there being many servicemen on board. *The Times* of 31 December described one of the trains involved as a workers' train. There were twenty-three deaths in the accident, which occurred near Eccles Station on the London Midland Railway.

One of the trains was the 6.30 am Rochdale to Pennington workers' train and the other, the 6.53 from Kenyon Junction to Manchester. They were travelling in opposite directions when the Rochdale engine hit the centre of the other train. Due to the war there were a number of local civil defence workers available to help with the rescue.

The Guardian of the same day had the headline: 'Workers' trains collide in the blackout'. They also had photographs and a diagram of how the accident occurred. They also mentioned how the blackout seemed to be forgotten after the crash, when bonfires were lit and torches used so that rescuers could see.

The inquiry under Major Wilson was opened very quickly and *The Times* reported on 8 January 1942 that visibility had been only 10 yards at the time of the crash. This was due to the weather as well as the blackout. There seems to have been some uncertainty between two signalmen as to which train was put onto which line at what time.

There was a serious accident in Scotland on 30 January 1942. Thirteen people were killed when the express from Edinburgh to Glasgow hit a light engine at Cowlairs, near Glasgow.

There was some doubt in *The Manchester Guardian* of 31 January when their headline claimed that there were eleven dead but the story said that eight

What looks like a serious accident in October 1943. There are no details of where this is.

were dead, based on a railway spokesman's report. It was later reported that eleven died.

The train was slowing up as it neared Glasgow at 5.00 pm. The first coach was smashed to matchwood and the next two were wrecked. There were again a number of servicemen on the train who helped the trapped and injured, and they used their field dressings in treating the injuries. A number of Polish soldiers on another train nearby also came to help.

There was some doubt as to the number of people killed in an accident at Ilford on 16 January 1944. *The Times* of 17 January had a headline that claimed fifteen were killed. This was based on a statement from the LNER that had at first only claimed one had died. In fact, only nine were killed. The accident involved two trains, both bound for Liverpool Street. One from Norwich ran into the back of one from Yarmouth at 7.15 pm. Most of the casualties were in the rear carriage of the Yarmouth train. It was a strange coincidence that serious accidents occurred at Ilford in both the First World War and in the Second World War.

The injured were treated by civil defence rescue squads. They were also helped by both British and American soldiers. *The Guardian* of 17 January said that there were a number of British and American soldiers on the platform at the time of the crash. There had also been a number of Americans on the train, no doubt from the numerous American bases in East Anglia. *The Guardian* reported that one injured American said that he would still get to Berlin. Much of the wreckage was strewn across the station platforms.

The following day, the 18 January, *The Manchester Guardian* told of an ARP worker who had died after running from his post towards the crash; he ran into a wall and later died of his injuries. Another fatality was Captain Frank Heilgers, the ex-MP for Bury St Edmunds.

A report on the inquest appeared in *The Times* on 4 February. It took place at East Ham and concerned the six British people killed in the accident. The other three people who died were American servicemen; a number of Americans had also been taken to hospital. The jury considered that the accident was due to the inefficient system of detonators working between Shenfield and Ilford. Detonators are an explosive charge that explode when a train runs over them and should be heard by the driver.

A LNER official said that as it was foggy two sections of the line were kept open between trains. This meant that two detonators were put on the line by the lever that put a signal at danger. The signalman at Seven Kings said that the Norwich train should have stopped at the danger signal before the station. When it passed through Seven Kings Station he knew something had gone wrong. He then phoned the signalman at Ilford, who also tried to stop the Norwich train. The driver later said he had seen no danger signals. The coroner told him that if he could see no signals he should assume they were at danger.

The Ministry of Transport report said that the fog came in rapidly and was very dense. It affected the view of the signals and although a fog man did arrive at the signal, it was ten minutes after the collision took place. The report also mentioned that due to which side the signals were on, reading them was often left to the fireman.

The loads carried by goods trains during the war could be a danger in themselves. When a goods train drove towards Soham Station on 2 June 1944 it was carrying a large number of bombs for American aircraft. There was an explosion at the station, which destroyed much of the station itself as well as a number of houses in the town, and it killed two people. It also put the town's gasworks out of action.

PS(¼) **SOUTHERN RAILWAY**

Circular to the staff of the Traffic and Locomotive Departments

in regard to

Fatal and Train Accidents, and Irregularities.

Set out below are brief particulars of the more important accidents and irregularities that have occurred for quarter ending 30th September, 1943, and it is hoped that they will be carefully read and that the lessons to be learnt therefrom will be of assistance to all staff concerned.

1. Fatal Accidents.

(a) At a halt station the Halt Keeper, after attending an up train, was making use of the staff crossing for the purpose of getting to the down platform when he was struck and killed by a fast train on the down line. Attention has been called in my previous Circulars to this type of accident, the present case being the third that has occurred this year from the same cause. These cases emphasise the great importance of the staff satisfying themselves beyond all doubt that the movement they are about to make across the lines can be carried out with safety.

(b) An unusual type of accident occurred to a driver of a steam train who, when passing another steam train on the opposite line, was struck in the head by the bunker of the other engine and killed instantly. The deceased was leaning well out of his cab with his head turned towards the rear of the engine, some detail of which he apparently wished to keep under observation and evidently did not realise the near approach of the train on the other line.

His exact intentions are unknown, as he did not say anything to his Fireman beforehand, nor did he take the precaution of first ascertaining that the opposite line was clear.

It can only be concluded that the deceased failed at the time to realise the danger in which he placed himself, in consequence of which he unfortunately omitted to take any steps to secure his own safety.

2. Train Accidents.

The number of train accidents that occurred in July was five, while twelve occurred in August and thirteen in September. Most of these cases were due to varying causes, many of which could have been avoided by the exercise of ordinary care and in a number of them much damage to stock and delay to traffic as a result of blockage of lines were caused. A number of them were however due to causes to which attention has previously been drawn, viz:—(a) vehicles standing astride of points and derailment resulting when the reverse movement was made, (b) signalmen prematurely moving points before vehicles had moved clear of connections and (c) vehicles after being shunted clear of connections not being properly secured and resulting in the vehicles moving back foul of other shunt movements. Special mention may be made of the following cases:—

(i) When a special freight train of 66 wagons and vans was leaving a yard for the down main line at a signal box where the Sykes Lock and Block system operates, the rearmost van became derailed at slip points (in the connection from yard to down main line) leading to the down local line, blocking the down main line; the train was brought to a stand after travelling a distance of 150 yards. This resulted in the down main line being put out of use for eight hours.

The derailment was due to the signalman operating the points leading to the down local line prematurely in readiness for a subsequent movement to that line when the freight train had passed. The back-lock release on the signal controlling the exit from the yard is given by the operation of a last vehicle treadle situated some distance from the down main line trailing points, and the signalman in an endeavour to expedite the working made use of the Sykes release key to free the back lock on the signal before the rear vehicle had passed clear of the points. The use of the key in this case was, of course, irregular and the signalman was acting against his own interests in destroying the safeguard for which the locking was specifically provided.

(ii) At a main line station a collision occurred at a fouling point of a connection from an up local to an up loop line between a light engine which had moved back on the loop line and an approaching train running on the up local line, resulting in derailment of the light engine and injuries to the enginemen of both engines.

A circular to staff on the Southern Railway from 1943. It lists fatal accidents that had occurred in the three-month run up to September 1943.

Fire on a goods train was dangerous at any time but when the first coach of the train caught fire as it approached the station and it was loaded with bombs it must have been terrifying for the driver. The driver and fireman acted with extreme bravery in unhooking the first coach and driving away from the rest of the train.

Train Accidents—*continued*.

The light engine had attached vehicles to a train standing at the up loop platform and in this position the engine stood the wrong side of the shunt signal controlling backward movements from the up loop line. The movement of the light engine was made as a result of the Fireman observing, as he alleged, the exhibition of a white light from the up loop platform which he interpreted as authority for the engine to move towards the fouling point and thence to the Locomotive Depot. A shunter was in charge of the light engine and it is established that no such hand signal as that alleged was exhibited neither had the shunter given any instructions to the driver to move as he was under the impression the light engine would remain where it stood until the shunt signal had been lowered.

The driver of the light engine was held responsible for failing to satisfy himself as to the position of the shunt signal, while the shunter was to blame for failing to instruct the driver what was the next move after detaching the engine from the vehicles.

This is a particularly bad case of lack of proper understanding between the shunter and driver and points to the need for special care in cases of the kind where engines have to stand temporarily on the wrong side of a shunt signal, and to the necessity for engines to move back to within the protection of such signals in order that the authorised movement can be made when the signal is lowered and the security of the interlocking assured.

8. **Irregularities.**

(*a*) A light engine came into contact with the up side gates at a public level crossing worked from a signal box where the signalman, after closing the gates across the roadway and lowering the down and up line signals for a down train and the light engine to pass, reversed the gates after the passing of the train and replaced all signals to danger as he thought he had sufficient time to allow a road vehicle to pass over the crossing before the arrival of the light engine; this engine, however, had already passed the up distant signal in the clear position and ran by the home and starting signals at danger. This is a case where the signalman took unnecessary risks and although the road vehicle which he intended should pass over the roadway between the two train movements had not in fact moved at the time of the "over-run" by the light engine the results might have been serious.

(*b*) An electric train was allowed to leave a block post while the section ahead was occupied by another train standing at the home signal of the signal box in advance. Train waiting apparatus is provided at the home signal in question but owing to a failure the presence of the train was not indicated in the box, the indicator standing at "Normal." The signalman at the box in advance, on receiving one beat on the block bell (which he assumed was the "call attention" signal for the following train) and being under the impression he had omitted to give "train out of section" for the first train telephoned to the rear signalman and enquired what train he had there; the latter replied that he had another train waiting without unfortunately designating the actual train. The signalman in advance thereupon gave the "train out of section" signal and accepted the second train; on lowering his home signal the first train which had been standing at that signal went forward which revealed the irregularity.

This case shows quite clearly how necessary it is for signalmen to come to a definite understanding when making train enquiries as to which particular train they are speaking about. Further, the sending of "one beat on the bell" (which, of course, is irregular) by the rear signalman was actually intended to call the advance man to the telephone and not as the "call attention" signal. In these two respects the advance signalman was misled.

(*c*) At a branch line station a collision between a passenger train and a shunting movement was narrowly averted when the Driver of the train passed the up home signal at danger at a time when the clearing point was obstructed by vehicles waiting to be shunted from the up to the down line through a crossover road situated to the rear of the up starting signal. A distance of 601 yards separates the up home and starting signals and the irregularity on the part of the Driver revealed that for some considerable time the Signalman had irregularly accepted up trains when the line was clear 440 yards ahead of the up home signal, instead of adopting the up starting signal as the clearing point in accordance with the standard block regulations.

No modification of the block regulation is authorised at the station in question and the irregular working had not been reported by the Station Master or other Supervisor.

The case points to the necessity for Station Masters and other Supervisors satisfying themselves from time to time that the regulations affecting block working, including any special instructions affecting the signalling of trains exhibited in Signal Boxes, are being strictly observed.

SAFETY FIRST.

R. M. T. RICHARDS,
Traffic Manager.

DEEPDENE HOTEL,
19th November, 1943.

The reverse of the staff circular. The circular states that signalmen must come to an understanding of which train they are talking about.

As they reached the station they called to the signalman to stop traffic coming the other way. Unfortunately, the coach exploded as they spoke to the signalman in the station. The fireman died instantly and the signalman the next day. Amazingly, the driver survived. The driver and fireman were later awarded the George Cross.

The Manchester Guardian reported on 3 June that the badly shattered market town of Soham was rife with stories of two brave railwaymen who drove a blazing wagon of bombs that cost one his life and badly injured the other.

The last serious accident of the war took place at London King's Cross on 4 February 1945. It involved the 6.00 pm train from Leeds, which went into a tunnel at the station but then began to move backwards. The last two coaches were derailed and one turned over. Two people died. One of the dead was Cecil Kimber, who had designed the MG motor car.

The Manchester Guardian of 5 February described the accident as a strange mishap. It described how the train left the station and was in the tunnel outside the station when for some unexplained reason it ran backwards. They also described Kimber as a well-known racing driver.

A few days later the newspaper described how the inquest at St Pancras had been adjourned by the coroner. This was because he wanted to know what happened because the public wanted to be reassured that it wouldn't recur.

CHAPTER 14

1945 to the Present Day

As many of the railway accidents that happened during the Second World War can be partly attributed to the blackout, one would think that once the war was over there would be fewer accidents. The technological advances made during the war period should also have had an influence on the occurrence of accidents. This proved not to be the case.

It was to be only a few months after hostilities ended before the first serious accident. It was another Scottish express on the London Midland and Scottish Railway on its way to London. It had been travelling overnight and at nine o'clock on the morning of 30 September 1945 at Bourne End it came off the line and ran into a field.

The Times of 1 October reported that twenty-eight bodies had been recovered but the death toll was expected to be heavier. They were correct in this as the final toll was forty-three. It was believed that the engine had fouled the points while changing from the fast to the slow line. This could have been due to the speed it was travelling at the time.

Rescue work was aided by American Air Force personnel from Bovington Air Base. Local villagers also helped by bringing refreshments left over from VE-Day celebrations to the rescue workers.

The next serious accident also occurred on the LMS. It was at Lichfield, when a fish train from Fleetwood to London ran into a passenger train that was standing in the station at 7.10 pm. There was a child killed on the engine of the fish train. The final death toll was twenty.

Once again the rescue work was aided by servicemen; members of the RAF and soldiers from the area were quickly on the scene. A number of the dead and injured were servicemen who had been on their way home after surviving the war. The town clerk of Lichfield, Mr A.N. Ballard, said it was

This crash seems to have caused plenty of damage to the carriage windows. It may be the Lichfield accident of 1946.

amazing that anyone on the passenger train had survived. Many of the injured had just got off the train and were hit by a carriage thrown onto the platform. No reason for the accident was given.

It was only a month after this accident that another occurred. It was on 10 February on the London North Eastern Railway at Potter's Bar, when a Newcastle-bound train from King's Cross hit a local train. This time there were only two deaths.

A spokesman for the company said that the 9.32 pm train from Hatfield to King's Cross was derailed near Potter's Bar and the 9.45 pm express ran into it. The two dead were both corporals – one from the Royal Engineers and the other from the Hertfordshire Regiment.

A soldier waiting at Potter's Bar said that the local train approached the station and seemed to hit the end of the platform he was waiting on. The wreckage was thrown across the tracks and then the express came and hit the wreckage.

Possibly another view of the Lichfield crash of 1946. It is interesting that a biplane is flying overhead.

The year of 1947 started badly when seven people died in an accident at Gidea Park in Essex. The 10.25 pm train from Liverpool Street to Southend was standing in Gidea Park Station when the 10.28 Liverpool Street to Peterborough train ran into the back of it after passing a signal in thick fog.

The last three coaches of the Southend train were destroyed; five people died instantly and two more later. There were forty-five injured. The guard on the Southend train had been just about to step on board when he heard the second train approaching, and he stayed on the platform.

Then, in a matter of two weeks, there were three fatal crashes, resulting in more than sixty deaths, so the accident at Gidea Park wasn't to be the only serious one of the year.

The first was on 24 October on the Southern Railway at Croydon. *The Times* of 25 October reported it was the worst accident in the history of the company. There were thirty-two deaths and nearly 200 injured. It happened at 8.30 am near South Croydon Station when two trains collided in thick fog.

The trains were the 7.33 from Hayward's Heath to London Bridge and the 8.04 from Tattenham Corner to London Bridge. The Hayward's Heath train had slowed down as it approached the station and the other train ran into it. Many of the passengers were children on their way to school. Both trains were very busy. There was no reason given for the accident in the early report.

Three days later the LNER Edinburgh to King's Cross express crashed at Goswick, near Berwick-on-Tweed. There were twenty-eight deaths. The early

There was another disaster in the fog in 1947 at Gidea Park. Seven people died in the accident.

Another view of the Gidea Park accident. In this image one of the carriages has hit the station roof.

Times report on 28 October said that there were still five people missing. The following day, *The Times* reported that six people thought to be missing had been found and were safe, although there were still thought to be other victims in the wreckage.

At the inquest in January it was claimed that notices had been sent out to everyone about repairs being carried out at Goswick. The signalman there said the accident had been caused by the train going too fast at a diversion. The driver of the train said he had seen no notices; otherwise he would have slowed down at Goswick.

Just over a week after the Goswick accident, on 6 November four more people died in a collision at Motspur Park in South London, on the Southern Railway. The 5.16 pm electric train from Waterloo to Chessington collided with the 4.45 electric train from Holmwood to London. The Waterloo train was full of homeward-bound workers.

Within two hours there was another collision on the Southern Railway at Herne Hill. A Blackfriars to Wimbledon electric train collided with a steam train from Ramsgate to Victoria. There was one death. Part of one carriage fell over a 30-foot embankment.

The accident that occurred on 23 June 1948 was due to an unusual cause. Twenty-four people died at Winsford, Cheshire, on the London Midland Railway. The 5.40 pm Glasgow to Crewe train stopped when someone pulled the communication cord. The guard ran back and put detonators on the line but it was too late to stop the Glasgow to Euston mail train from running into the back of the stationary train.

The inquiry was to concentrate on two points, according to *The Times* of 19 April: who pulled the communication cord and why there were two trains on the same stretch of line at the same time. According to *The Manchester Guardian* the police were seeking a man who ran away from the train. They believed he may have been a local man who pulled the cord so that he could take a shortcut home.

There was some respite before the next accident, which occurred on 27 August 1950 and led to six deaths. It involved an Irish mail train that was due to leave Holyhead at 1.45 am. The train hit a light engine near Penmaenmawr Station just after 3.00 am. The fireman of the train managed to stop a freight train carrying explosives before it ran into the back of the damaged train.

On 16 March 1951 the 10.06 am train from Doncaster to King's Cross collided with a bridge and twelve people died. The accident happened when the third coach of the train hit Balby Bridge just outside Doncaster Station. The coach then became jammed under the bridge.

One of the passengers in the coach said that the carriage began to sway and vibrate and another passenger told them to lift up their legs. Again, it seems to have been common knowledge that in accidents passengers' legs were often trapped between seats.

There was a strange report on the accident in *The Manchester Guardian* explaining that the public inquiry into the accident would only last one day and the evidence relating to the crash would all be heard in private. There was, perhaps, still a mood of secrecy left over from the war.

The Times of 22 September 1951 had a headline announcing that thirteen had died in a train wreck. In fact, there were fifteen deaths when the Liverpool to Euston express had left the rails and crashed down the embankment near Stowehill Tunnel at Weedon on the previous day.

The accident happened at eleven o'clock in the morning. Four Metropolitan Police sergeants were driving past to London from the police school at Rydon on Dunsmore, near Coventry. Three of them went to assist while the other went for help. A railway spokesman said that the track had been ripped up but this was not given as the reason for the derailment.

One of the kitchen staff on the train was trapped under an axle, according to *The Manchester Guardian*. They also mentioned how the Salvation Army had turned up and opened a mobile canteen for the injured and the rescue workers.

It was to be a year before the next serious accident – one of the worst to ever occur in Britain. There were 112 fatalities and more than 300 injured when the Perth to Euston express ran into a local train at Harrow and Wealdstone Station. Then a Euston to Manchester 0045 express ran into the wreckage. The damage was described as looking as if it had been caused by heavy bombing.

The accident happened at 8.20 am on 8 October 1952. The following day *The Times* reported that eighty-five were dead and 170 injured. The Perth train had been running an hour late when it ran into the local train from Tring to Euston, which was standing at the station platform. It was less than a minute later that the Euston to Manchester ran into the wreckage.

As well as passengers on the trains there were also casualties amongst those waiting on the platforms. One passenger said that the carriage he was in was suspended 20 feet in the air after the collision. He could hear screams from the carriage below the one he was in. *The Times* reported wreckage standing at up to 30 feet high.

The whole of platform six was turned into a first aid station. It was manned by a large number of American airmen along with nurses and volunteers.

Blood, plasma and morphine was flown in to Northolt from the US air base at Burtonwood, Lancashire, to help with treatment of the injured.

The Ministry of Transport report was written by Lieutenant Colonel Wilson, who stated that the driver of the Perth train did not reduce speed at the signal. The levels of visibility varied due to thick fog. There was no blame put on the signalmen.

The next accident was also in London when two trains collided at 7.00 pm in a tunnel on the Central Line between Stratford and Leyton, on 8 April 1953. Twelve people died in the accident.

The two trains were the Ealing Broadway to Epping and the Greenford to Hainault. Both were due at Stratford within two minutes of each other. The first train was stationary when the second one ran into it. Automatic signalling was in operation when the accident occurred. Due to the narrow tunnel where the accident happened it was very difficult to get stretcher cases out. There were reports of children's voices still being heard in the wreckage seven hours after the crash.

On 15 August 1953 there was a collision between an electric and a steam train near Manchester. There were ten deaths, many due to a carriage from the electric train that fell from Irk Valley Viaduct into a river below. It happened at eight o'clock in the morning. The headline in *The Manchester Guardian* stated: 'Ten killed as trains collide on a viaduct'.

The electric train had been travelling from Bury to Manchester, the steam train from Manchester to Bacup. The viaduct where the collision took place was about a mile from Manchester's Victoria Station. The steam train was crossing the path of the electric train when they collided. The first carriage of the electric train went through the wall of the viaduct and hung over the edge, held by its coupling. It looked as though the whole train may have gone over but the first coach broke free and fell.

Rescue workers had to stand in water up to their shoulders to release the injured and retrieve the bodies of the dead. It was eleven hours before the carriage could be retrieved from the river.

There was a derailment on 23 January 1955 at Sutton Coalfield. Seventeen people died in the accident, which happened when the 12.15 pm York to Bristol express was directed onto a loop line because of repairs to the main line. The train was derailed when it was passing through the station.

One of the passengers said that some of his fellow travellers were thrown up and hit the roof. A Royal Marine travelling in one carriage had been asleep and woke up on the track. The carriage roof had been ripped off. An RAF pilot officer was also thrown out of his carriage. He heard a child screaming and was told that it was a 7-year-old boy who had been travelling alone. He could not get him out. There was a 19-year-old RAF airman returning to his base at Locking, Somerset. He said that the carriage was dragged along the sleepers. He then pulled twenty people out of the wreckage.

The year 1955 was turning out to be a bad one for the railways. On 20 November eleven people died near Didcot, in Berkshire (now in Oxfordshire). The train was an excursion from South Wales to Paddington. The engine came off the line and fell down an embankment, taking four coaches with it, which were badly damaged.

As with other recent accidents military help was at hand. The embankment where the accident occurred was alongside the RAF depot at

A serious accident that involved at least two trains. Unfortunately, there is nothing on the photo to show where this is. OBVIOUSLY HARROW + WEALDSTONE

Milton. RAF men were joined by soldiers from the Army ordnance depot at Didcot. The report in *The Manchester Guardian* on 21 November said that the total number of dead was still unknown. A ticket collector and a child were thought to be still trapped in the wreckage.

It was less than two weeks before another serious accident occurred and this time the old enemy of the train crash was involved. Part of the train caught fire. The accident took place on 2 December 1955 at Barnes. Twelve people died in the accident when a Southern Railway electric train ran into a goods train.

The electric passenger train was the 11.12 pm from Waterloo to Windsor and the goods train the 10.50 from Battersea to Brent. The front coach of the electric train hit the rear of the goods train and then, according to a witness, burst instantly into flames. A local man who saw the crash said that there were screams coming from the coach but the fire was too fierce for them to get anywhere near it to help. *The Guardian* repeated the news that rescuers were beaten back by the flames. They also said that the fire was so fierce it burnt holes in the bridge over the line.

A man who was in the first coach said that it turned over but didn't catch fire for about five minutes, and this happened after an explosion. Then the doors, which were now above him, were forced open and he and others in the coach were pulled out.

The next serious accident to occur was almost exactly two years after the last one and was again in London. Ninety deaths resulted from an accident on 4 December 1957 at Lewisham. *The Times* of 5 December gave the number of dead as fifty-two. Two trains had collided in thick fog between St John's and Lewisham stations. The wreckage then struck a viaduct above the crash, which had a train on it at the time. The viaduct then collapsed.

The trains involved were the 4.56 pm steam train from Cannon Street to Ramsgate, which crashed into the back of the 5.18 electric Charing Cross to Hayes train. The Nunhead flyover then collapsed onto the rear of the Cannon Street train. The 5.22 Holborn Viaduct to Dartford, which was on the flyover, was derailed.

There were an estimated 2,000 people on the three trains. There were so many injured that the three nearest hospitals reached a point where they could not take any more. The injured were then sent to hospitals as far away as Bromley. Rescue workers carried on, despite the danger of the viaduct above them falling down. Due to the danger from the viaduct it took four hours to get all the injured out. A woman in one of the carriages of the electric train said that it toppled over and everyone was thrown into a struggling mass of arms and legs. The silence was then broken by a man who said, 'Let's have cigarettes all round.'

The year 1958 was to prove a bit safer on Britain's railways but it didn't start off that way. On 30 January ten people died in a collision at Dagenham East Station when two trains collided. It seems that one of the trains passed a red signal in thick fog and ran into the back of another train.

The Manchester Guardian reported how people in the neighbouring houses were the first on the scene. One local said that many of the passengers in the front coaches of the first train were unhurt and went to bus stops and continued on their way home.

The Times of 1 February carried the headline: 'Crash line had automatic control'. The story went on to quote the Minister of Transport, who reminded all British Rail staff of the difficult burden that fell on them when operating trains in heavy fog. There was also a comment from Mr J. Watkins, a member of the Transport Commission, who said it was natural that the public should be concerned about the number of recent accidents, especially after 1956, when no one had been killed in rail accidents.

Watkins commented that, with the number of journeys undertaken on the railways in Britain, the chance of dying in a rail accident was about one in 24 million journeys. He also explained how new electrical and mechanical safeguards against human error were being introduced, costing about £150 million. The line where the Dagenham accident happened had the Hudd system of automatic train control and the control equipment on the engine involved would have been in working order when it went into service. This then wouldn't have actually given the public a lot of confidence in the new system if it had already been working at the time of the accident.

The Ministry of Transport report written by Brigadier Langley said that the automatic train control had been working on both engines. Both trains had also only been travelling slowly, the first at 5 miles an hour, the second at 20 miles an hour. The driver of the second train was inexperienced and had never travelled the route in fog. Langley commented that the driver probably missed the signal due to the poor visibility.

Fog played a part in a number of accidents of around this time. It was a serious problem, especially in London, with thick smog that made visibility extremely difficult, not only on the railways but on the roads and even on the pavements.

The next serious accident of the year was at Eastbourne Station, where five people died on 25 August. The accident involved a collision between an electric train and an express. It happened at 7.32 am when the 6.47 electric

A large number of people have turned out to help clear debris, but again there is nothing to show where this accident occurred.

train from Ore to London Bridge was standing at the platform. The express was from Glasgow. It appeared that the electric train was late and the express early.

There were a number of witness statements in *The Times*'s report of 26 August about what happened to them. Apart from the running times of the trains, however, there was no reason given as to why the accident happened.

Over the following few years there was some respite from serious accidents and the next one did not happen until 21 January 1960, when a goods train ran into a passenger train near Settle Station. Five people died. The passenger train was a Glasgow to London Express and the goods train was the 1.45 pm from Leeds to Carlisle.

The Times of 22 January gave the reason for the accident as the engine of the goods train becoming derailed and hitting the coaches of the passenger train. The track was damaged by the connecting rod of the engine on the passenger train coming loose, which then caused the derailment of the approaching goods train.

The Times of 17 July 1961 had a headline that said: 'Holiday diesel leapfrogs'. Not only was it another holiday train accident, it was also one of the first to mention a diesel engine. Although diesel engines had been used before the First World War they had not been widely used in Britain before the Second World War. It was only in the 1960s that they began to steadily replace steam engines.

The accident on 16 July 1961 happened at Singleton Bank, near Blackpool. Seven people died when the diesel train bound for the Isle of Man boat at Fleetwood hit a stationary goods train at 10.25 am. The ballast workers who had been with the goods train were almost crushed as the passenger train leapfrogged the goods train and fell down the bank where they were working. According to *The Guardian,* the train had braked for 800 yards before the collision took place. As all phone lines were down police radios had to be used to contact the emergency services.

A bus that arrived to pick up the railway workers was instead used to carry those injured who could sit to hospital. Although the danger of gas lighting causing fire was long gone, *The Times*'s report stated that diesel fumes threatened to burst into flames and one man was overcome by the vapours.

There was another accident involving a diesel train on 3 June 1962. Three people were killed when the 10.15 pm train from King's Cross to Edinburgh broke in two. The coaches, which were all sleeping cars, overturned. The passengers included a group of Conservatives who had been to the wedding of Mr Patrick Wolrige-Gordon MP in Suffolk.

The train had been diverted because of maintenance work on the main line. There were speed restrictions in force on the track where the accident happened. As the passengers had been in bed when the accident took place calls for clothes went out, as many had left theirs in the train.

For the first time in the past few years there were two fatal accidents in a year in 1962. The second took place on Boxing Day at Coppenhall Junction, near Winsford. The Glasgow to Euston Express ran into the rear of another train, killing eighteen and injuring many others. *The Guardian* said that the automatic warning system had no bearing on the accident.

The Times published a report on 5 January 1963 with the headline: 'Rail crash driver ignored rule when halted'. The driver of the express admitted at the enquiry that after stopping at a red signal neither he nor his fireman could get through to the signal box on the phone. The train was already late so he passed the signal at caution. As he moved forward the next signal changed to yellow but then they saw another train.

The inquiry was then told that a circuit of sixteen phones in the area were all out of order at the time. The driver said that his train was only travelling at a crawl at the time of the collision. There was also some dispute about a half-hour gap between the signalman at Winsford signal box receiving a phone call about the accident and the 999 call.

The driver was asked about rule fifty-five, which was about passing a danger signal when the phone was not working. He said that the rule meant he was to stand at a signal for two or three minutes and then carry on, providing the way was clear to the signal ahead. The driver said that he had proceeded consistent with the rules.

The accident that occurred on 15 August 1963 was unusual in that the only three fatalities were railway employees. It happened at Knowle and Doridge Station when the Birmingham to Paddington express ran into the rear of a car transporter train. The fatalities were all on the express and were the driver and co-driver of the diesel engine, along with another man. Lunch was being served on the express and crockery was thrown about when the trains collided. A chef on the train was also injured.

The Ministry of Transport report was written by Colonel D. McMullen. He found the cause was that the signalman obstructed the line with a train being shunted after giving the all-clear signal to the express.

Three people died in an accident at Cheadle Hume on 28 May 1964. *The Times* of 29 May ran the headline: 'Three die in school outing rail crash'. Two of the dead were girls of seven and eight. The train was from Stafford and was going to York. The children were to visit the railway museum and the Minster and have a trip on the river.

Part of the train was derailed on a bridge that had a speed limit of 10 miles per hour. This was a temporary structure and was in place while the road was being widened. The bridge was damaged in the accident; it was fortunate that the train did not fall onto the road underneath it. A teacher in one of the coaches that was overhanging the bridge's edge ordered the children in the carriage to the side to try and balance it.

On 17 December 1965 the driver and co-driver of an empty passenger train died in a collision at Bridgend. The train hit a landslide of rock and debris that had blocked the line.

After several years of very few serious accidents, 1967 was to be a turning point. The first of a number of accidents took place on 28 February, when nine people died at Stechford, near Birmingham. There was a collision between a diesel engine and an electric train. The train was the Manchester to Coventry passenger train.

The accident occurred on a stretch of line that, according to *The Times*, was

This shows the Tollerton crash of June 1950. Much of the side of this carriage has been ripped off. (www.transporttreasury.co.uk)

controlled by a new electronic signal box at New Street Station said to be the most up to date in Britain. The diesel engine was shunting near the scene of the accident when the collision occurred. The enquiry into the accident was to be held at Birmingham under Colonel D. McMullen, the chief inspector of railways.

Less than a week later, on 5 March, there was another fatal accident, at Connington South. Five people died when a train came off the tracks. There was some doubt as to the cause but in a report in *The Times* on 7 March it was stated that a piece of metal found amongst the wreckage may give a clue.

The metal was a missing section of buckeye coupling from the front of the carriage in which most of the injuries took place. It was also mentioned that there had been two other crashes in the past five years on the same stretch of straight level track. *The Guardian* reported that the inspector of the permanent way told the London inquiry that they were baffled by the reasons for the crash.

On the same day, 7 March, *The Times* published an article entitled 'No evidence that the railways are getting less safe'. The article asked whether with two fatal accidents in a week, the British Railways Board were skimping on inspection and maintenance to save money. The writer put this question to the senior officials of British Rail.

The answer was that the relationship between the number of accidents to the number of train journeys showed that it was a very safe means of travel. There was, however, an upward trend – about 100 a year – in accidents caused by malicious acts such as obstructions being placed on the line. There were also a number of derailments involving freight trains using old-fashioned short-wheel base wagons.

There was a noticeable tendency for every fifth year to be a bad one for railway accidents and 1967 seemed to be one of those years. On 31 July seven people died at Thirsk when a goods train was derailed and a train on the opposite line ran into it. According to *The Times* on 1 April, the passenger train was ripped open by the goods train. It was as if a can opener had been taken to the carriages, said one passenger on the train.

The accident was reported in a novel fashion. The pilot of a Provost jet aircraft on a training flight saw it and reported it by radio to the RAF base at Topcliffe. Twenty airmen were then sent to help.

The express train had been travelling at about 75 to 80 miles an hour when the driver saw the derailed train. He said that he applied the brakes and shut his eyes. He was unhurt, as were the crew of the goods train.

The Guardian published a photograph of the wreck that showed passengers searching through it for their luggage. Geoffrey Rhodes, MP for Newcastle East, called for an inquiry on the London to Edinburgh line, where there had been three bad accidents.

Bad luck on the railways continued when, in the same year, one person died at Foxhall Junction on 27 September. Even worse, on 5 November forty-nine people died at Hither Green in an accident due to a derailment at high speed and ten of the twelve coaches turned over. *The Times* of 6 November mentioned in the headline that the accident occurred only a mile from the site of the Lewisham accident that happened in 1957.

The accident occurred at 9.16 pm. The first two coaches had travelled on, staying on the line, whilst the rest of the train came off and turned over. Two of the carriages were on a bridge over St Mildred's Road. Just as in accidents of the Victorian period, hundreds of sightseers turned up to watch the rescue work. The police had to tell them to go home. According to *The Guardian* the train derailed in heavy rain and most of the casualties were in the fourth, fifth and sixth coaches.

The Ministry of Transport report stated that the rail fractured under the train and that the third coach was derailed. The broken section was a shortened length of rail between a continuous welded rail. The concrete sleeper under the joint had been replaced with a wooden one. Colonel Dennis McMullen, chief inspecting officer of the railways, who wrote the report, said that the fracture occurred due to unsatisfactory support under the joint.

The Dagenham crash occurred in January 1958. Again, it was a collision in fog, and ten people died.

The Times of 16 November reported that deaths by train accidents were at a ten-year high in 1967. There had been eighty-two people killed. Colonel McMullen described it as a most distressing year. His annual report stated that instances of broken rails continued to increase and were the main cause of the accidents.

According to *The Times*'s report McMullen called for continuous welded track to replace jointed track. British Rail said they were installing welded track at a cost of £15 million a year. McMullen went on to blame the increase in accidents on the changeover to diesel engines that were pulling old trucks at higher speeds.

In spite of the five-year trend, the number of fatal accidents did not decline in 1968, although the number of people killed in each accident wasn't as high as had recently been the case. The year began badly with an accident on 6 January at Hixon, in Staffordshire, where eleven people died.

The accident was due to a train hitting a large transporter lorry carrying a 120-ton transformer on a level crossing. It was an unmanned crossing and there was a sign just before it saying that drivers of heavy loads should phone the signalman before crossing. The lorry carrying the transformer had a police

Another view of the Dagenham crash. As well as ten dead there were eighty injured.

BRITAIN'S RAILWAY DISASTERS

escort. It was only halfway across before the crossing lights began to flash and a train came.

The Guardian of 7 January headlined that twelve had died as an express train hit a giant lorry crossing the lines, and carried a diagram of how the crossing operated.

Automatic half-barriers at level crossings had been introduced in 1961 and according to British Rail these were the safest form of level crossing in the world. They had been in use for many years in Europe and the US, with very few accidents, and this was the case if all the regulations were observed, they stated.

The Times's report of 8 January mentioned a number of recent accidents where car drivers had tried to zigzag round the barriers after they had come down and had then been hit by trains. The article asked if the regulations had been followed in the case of this latest accident. There was some doubt as to whether anyone connected with the large load had telephoned the signalman before they attempted to cross the lines.

Claims about the safety of automatic crossings were beginning to look a bit less believable when, on 16 April at Beckingham, five people died on an automatic level crossing. All five fatalities were in a car hit by a train on the crossing after it stalled halfway across.

There was one more fatal accident in 1968 but this time it was due to a fire. The 7.40 am from Bedford to St Pancras caught fire on 30 August. It was a diesel engine and *The Times*'s report of 31 August said that this was the fourth incident of its kind to occur on this line.

Passengers broke windows and jumped out of the train after the communication cord was pulled and the train stopped. The minister of transport, Baron Richard Marsh, said that at no time did the fire enter the carriages so the injuries and the two deaths were due to passengers jumping out of the train. It seems that the danger of fire from gas in early trains had now been replaced with danger from fire due to diesel.

The year 1969 was to see a number of fatal accidents although the numbers killed were lower than they had been in previous years. On 4 January four people died in a collision between a passenger and a goods train in fog at Marden, in Kent. The passenger train was a London to Ramsgate express.

The Times of 6 January reported that there had been a build-up of traffic on the line due to a signal failure at Marden. The system of coloured light signals, visible in fog, should have kept the line behind the goods train clear for 3 miles. British Rail was, according to the report, going to trial an automatic warning system in the area. With this system the driver would be given visible and audible warning of danger ahead. If a stop signal was passed then the train would automatically be stopped. It had not been used in the Southern Region before due to the great deal of traffic operating on the system.

On 8 April two people died at Monmore Green, near Wolverhampton. It was once again a collision between a passenger and a goods train. According to *The Times,* the passenger train was on the wrong line although rail officials had previously claimed it was on the correct line. It had, in fact, left the up line about half a mile from the crash site.

The passenger train was an electric train and the goods train was drawn by a diesel engine. The engine and the first carriage of the electric train were destroyed and the drivers of both trains died.

The worst crash of the year was on 7 May, when six people died at Morpeth. The train was an express from London to Aberdeen. The reason

This was an accident that took place in October 1959 at Smedley Viaduct, Manchester.

was suspected to be an obstruction on the line but the fact that the engine stayed on the line seemed to disprove this. The other possible reason was perhaps the excessive speed of the train on a stretch of line where there was a speed limit.

The Guardian of 8 May reported that the British Rail inquiry on the Morpeth accident would begin that day at Newcastle. A Mr Marsh said that there would be a public enquiry within two weeks. There was a search still taking place for one of the survivors. He was a member of the Royal Scots Regiment who had been under arrest on the train for desertion and had used the accident as an opportunity to escape.

The following year, 1970, was to be a much safer one for rail travellers. The only fatal crash occurred on 20 May. Two people died when the middle coaches of a Manchester to Hadfield train became derailed. It was believed that the points were changed under the train by mistake as the train passed over them.

The next fatal accident occurred on 2 July 1971, when a school excursion train was derailed at Tattenhall Junction, near Chester, and two children died. There were about 400 children on the train on their way home to Birmingham from Wales. The cause of the accident was a buckled track.

The next serious accident also involved an excursion train. An outing of the Kentish Town Railwaymen's Club was derailed at Eltham Well Hall in South London on its way back from Margate. It was believed that the train came off the rails as it came round a curve at too high a speed. Six people died. A team of army surgeons from the Royal Herbert Military Hospital at Shooter's Hill came to help. Not everyone at the scene was there to help as three youths were arrested for looting the possessions of the injured.

Another fatal accident occurred on 30 August 1973, at Shield's Junction, near Glasgow, when two passenger trains collided. Overhead power lines fell onto the wreckage and caused a fire – another way that trains tended to catch fire in railway accidents. Five people died.

The engines were an electric from Wemyss Bay and a diesel from Ayr. They were both going in the same direction on the same line when the collision occurred, the electric train hitting the rear of the diesel. A passenger in the front carriage of the electric train told how it caught fire while within 8 feet of the diesel engine and there was oil running out of it.

There seemed to be another five-year cycle of rail accidents occurring. The next fatal accident, on the 19 December 1973, had the highest death toll since 1968. Ten people died at Ealing. The train was the 5.18 pm from Paddington to Oxford, full of workers and Christmas shoppers on their way home.

By this time the reports on rail accidents in *The Times* named the writer of the article. The report on this accident stated that the reason that the train had become derailed was not known. No other train was involved but there were reports of the train wobbling as it went over a set of points.

The Guardian report stated that seven were killed in a derailment on the 'trouble line'. There had been three accidents on the line in the past six weeks. It was thought that this one may have been caused by vandals putting something on the line.

The Ministry of Transport report found that the accident had not been due to vandalism but that the rearmost battery box door on the engine was unlocked. It had opened as the train moved and hit objects along the rails. This was what led to the derailment but there was no certainty as to who had left the box open.

When an Underground train crashed at Moorgate on 28 February 1975 it was at first feared that the number of dead was at least twenty-nine. That was according to a report in *The Times* on 1 March. In fact, the total number of fatalities was forty-three.

The wreckage of the crash at Turvey in 1960. (George Smith, www.transporttreasury.co.uk)

211

The rush-hour train had run into a dead-end tunnel and caused the first three carriages to become telescoped. Freeing those trapped in the train was very difficult due to the restricted space and the darkness of the tunnel. A police officer described it as like working in sardine can. It was twelve hours before all the trapped were freed and it was described as the worst accident in the 100 years of the London Underground system.

The Guardian headline declared: 'Experts sift the evidence'. There seemed no explanation as to how the train had gone through a sand trap and the buffers to hit a wall. London Underground Operations Manager Mr Grahame Bruce thought that the brakes must not have been applied. Even if something had happened with the driver, then the dead man's handle should have worked to stop the train. It was claimed that the Tube was one of the safest underground railways in the world: there had been only fourteen deaths in rail accidents since 1938. Twelve of these had occurred more than twenty years earlier.

On 6 June 1975 a Euston to Glasgow sleeper express was derailed at Trent Valley Station at Nuneaton, killing six. There was a 20-mile an hour speed limit at the station while old lines and new lines were being linked. Witnesses said that the train was travelling much faster than 20 miles an hour. The British Rail divisional manager at Stoke-on-Trent told a press conference that the track running through the station was unsuitable for high-speed running. He also claimed that the driver would have known about the speed limit.

The Guardian of 8 June reported that the Department of the Environment had been trying for years to persuade British Rail to make radical changes to its method of warning drivers about speed restrictions. This was now likely to be enforced due to the Nuneaton crash.

There was a repeat of the past for victims of the accident on 6 July 1978. Twelve people died at Taunton when the Penzance to London sleeper train caught fire. David Penhaligon, MP for Truro, told the Commons that when he used the sleeper train, all doors on the carriages were locked. *The Guardian* reported that there were gasps in the House as this was revealed.

The locking of carriage doors was something that had been complained about more than a century before. As well as the doors being locked, the windows were double glazed and could not be opened. A manager from British Rail claimed that doors out of the carriages should not have been locked.

The Times's report of 7 July said that it was at first believed that a problem with the wiring in one of the old carriages had caused the fire. The wiring was, however, checked monthly. The Ministry of Transport report found that the fire had been started by bags of linen left against a heater. The locked doors had led to problems evacuating the train but there was no evidence that this had led to loss of life. Major King, who wrote the report, found that the training of sleeping car attendants was unsatisfactory. There was also no means of raising the alarm on the train.

On 19 December 1978 the 23.20 electric train from Victoria to Brighton stopped at a signal near Patcham Tunnel. It was then hit by the 21.40 electric train from Victoria to Littlehampton. Three people died.

On 16 April there was a collision at Gilmour Street Station at Paisley. The 19.50 Glasgow to Wemyss Bay train was hit by an Ayr to Glasgow train and seven people died. The accident was caused by what was known as the 'ding ding and away' system, which was changed after this. This was a slang term for the driver receiving a flag or bell signal to make him go even if the signal was at danger. According to *The Guardian*, the train was full of Easter day-trippers returning from the Ayrshire coast.

The last serious accident of the year was on 22 October, at Invergowrie, when five people died. A train stopped due to a problem on board. Then a following train ran into the back of it. *The Times* of 15 November reported that the signalling system at the scene of the crash was of a higher standard than was normal for such a line.

The inquiry was told that the Glasgow to Aberdeen express ran into a Glasgow to Aberdeen train that was stationary. Two of the coaches from the stationary train were thrown onto the mud of the Tay Estuary. *The Guardian* report said that the first train had been in difficulties for several minutes before it stalled. There was a suspicion that the second train had been trying to push the stalled train on to a safer position.

It was to be more than two years before there was another fatal accident on the railways. On 11 December 1981 four people died at Seer Green when two trains collided while on the same stretch of track.

There was some dispute over the cause of the accident and in *The Times*'s report of 8 January 1982 it was stated that British Rail were considering action against the signalman involved. Meanwhile, the parents of two boys who died in the crash were considering taking action against BR, but not against the signalman.

The signalman had been praised for his frankness by the Department of Transport inquiry. They said his mistake had not made the accident inevitable. He had allowed two trains onto the same section of track but the weather and speed of the trains had contributed to what had happened. *The Guardian* report claimed that one train had been a rush-hour passenger train while the

The side of the carriage has been completely ripped off in this accident of January 1960. (www.transporttreasury.co.uk)

other was engaged in maintenance. It had it stopped to clear a fallen tree and was hampered by deep snow drifts.

There were also calls for radio links to be installed on all trains. It was described as 'nineteenth-century' that the signalman had to shout at the guard on the passing train to give warning. Britain was well behind other countries in the use of radios on trains. There was some dispute as to whether this was due to cost or union opposition.

There was a relatively long gap between the last and the next serious accident. It was on 30 July 1984, when thirteen people died in the Polmont rail accident. A rush-hour train between Edinburgh and Glasgow came off the line after hitting a cow. According to *The Times* of 31 July, it was the worst disaster for seventeen years, although I'm not sure how they came to this conclusion when the Moorgate accident, where forty-three died, had been eleven years before this, unless they weren't including it because it was on the London Underground.

It seems hard to believe that such devastation could have been caused by a train hitting a cow, even if it was travelling at 80 miles an hour. The leading coach was apparently thrown over onto its roof and others were thrown off the tracks. Although the remains of a cow were found, a British Rail spokesman said that it could not be said that this was definitely the cause.

The Guardian of 1 August also described the accident as the worst for seventeen years and posed a question about the safety aspects of push and pull trains relating to the positioning of the diesel engines. It was hoped that this would be examined in a public enquiry.

A later report in *The Times*, of 22 August, claimed that the accident had been due to people who removed sections of fencing so they could cross the line. It seems then that the cause *had* been the train hitting a cow. There were a number of gaps in the fencing along the railway in the area and cows often got onto the line.

The Ministry of Transport report was written by Major King, who said that between 1 January 1974 and 31 December 1984 there had been 1,096 collisions of trains with animals. This was about 100 a year and two-thirds of these involved cows or bulls. This had led to twenty-four derailments.

The lengthening time between fatal railway accidents came to an abrupt end as there were three fatal crashes in 1984. The next to occur was at Wembley on 11 October. Three people died after a collision when a train passed a danger signal. The accident involved a Euston to Bletchley train, which hit a goods train. In a report in *The Times* on 16 February 1985 it was claimed that the driver of the passenger train had a forty-five second blank in his memory of the period just before the crash.

The Guardian also published a discussion as to whether the Wembley accident was due to a fault in the signalling system or human error. The reports in *The Guardian* now also included the name of the reporter.

A damaged engine at the Swindon Works in 1961. (George Smith, www.transporttreasury.co.uk)

The last fatal crash of the year was on 4 December, when three people died at Eccles as two trains collided. A passenger train ran into the back of a petrol tanker train. *The Times* of 6 December reported that a passenger at Eccles Station had seen the passenger train go through red signals. A British Rail spokesman claimed that a signalman may also have seen the train pass a red signal.

The Guardian explained that a report on the Eccles crash could take more than a year to complete. This was due to the sad catalogue of accidents afflicting British Rail over the past twelve months. The Department of Transport was, it claimed, anxious over the sudden spate of accidents after five years of safe travel.

There was another fatal accident involving a level crossing on 26 July 1986. Nine people died at Lockington, near Hull, when a Bridlington to Hull train hit a vehicle on the crossing. There was a denial by British Rail that the warning lights at the crossing had not been working. Although it was normally the occupants of the vehicle on the crossing at most danger in such a collision, the first coach of the train was jack-knifed back onto itself, killing a number of passengers.

Alongside the report of the accident in *The Times* of 28 July was an admission by British Rail that the difference between open crossings such as the one where the accident occurred and one with barriers was cost. They did not declare though that either type was safer than the other. There were at this time still around 500 crossings that were worked by a man who opened and shut crossing gates and who lived by the crossing, but these were being phased out. *The Guardian* said that MPs had called for an inquiry into unmanned crossings. Doctor John Marek, MP for Wrexham, claimed that the government was putting lives at risk by encouraging cheap crossings.

On 19 October 1987 four people were killed after a bridge was washed away on the river Towy in Wales and a train fell into the river. The river was swollen due to high rainfall. The train was the 5.20 am from Swansea to Shrewsbury. The bridge had still been in place when the train began to cross but collapsed as the train was travelling over it. There were British Rail officials on board the train to check the safety of the line. It was claimed that it was normal procedure for the first train of the day to be used to check the safety of a line. The water authority said that the river would not reach such a high level more than once in a 100 years.

The Guardian of 20 October mentioned that British Rail was aware of a possible problem with the bridge but that it looked fine in the dark. Two days later they reported that more than half of the derailments and collisions on the railway were caused by human error and an increasing number of signals were being passed at red.

The Ministry of Transport report was written by A. Cooksey; it denied rumours that the train was being used to test a suspect bridge. It also denied reports that the Welsh water authority had released water from a reservoir, making the flood worse.

Cooksey found that the collapse was due to the failure of a bridge pier, which was undermined by the scouring action of the river, and that it was also an abnormally high flood for the river Towy.

One of the worst losses of life in recent times on the railways occurred at London's King's Cross Station on 18 November 1987, but this was not due to a train accident. A fire began on an escalator in the station at around 7.30 pm and resulted in the deaths of thirty-one people. Being a major station on the London Underground with a number of lines running through it, as well as being a main line station, there were naturally many people passing through at the time.

The fire was believed to have been started by a match dropped onto the escalator serving the Piccadilly Line. Many people were trapped underground by the fire and some escaped by getting on trains that were still running through the station.

The accident at Cheadle Hulme of May 1964, in which three people died.

The fire was at first very small and was examined by staff and police who then called the fire brigade. The decision to evacuate the station was taken at 7.39 pm. The fire brigade arrived but by 7.45 the fire had spread and become out of control. Smoke began to fill the station and this was what killed many of the victims.

The public enquiry found that staff had been given little training to deal with fire as this scale of catastrophe had never happened on the Underground system before. Police officers trying to help an injured man escape found themselves trapped by a locked gate. It was only when a cleaner opened the gate leading to the Midland City platforms that they were able to get out.

The dead included a fireman, Station Officer Colin Townsley, who was in command of the first pump to arrive at the scene. It was thought that he had stopped to help a passenger in difficulty. One of the victims was not identified until January 2004.

A number of the worst rail accidents in the previous few years had been in London, the scene of another accident on 12 December 1988, when thirty-five people died. Two trains collided at Clapham Junction and then a third ran into the wreckage. A faulty signal was blamed.

The driver of a commuter train had stopped his train and left the cab to report the faulty signal and an express train then ran into the back of the stationary train. A number of passengers who were either thrown clear or climbed out of the wreckage were then hit by an empty train that was passing on another line. The signals were apparently temporary ones and were not working properly.

The Guardian reported that the accident was the worst for twenty years and the signal was blamed. MPs demanded to know if there was any link between the accident and financial restraints placed on British Rail.

Less than three months later, on 4 March 1989, five people died in the Purley Station crash. A train missed a signal and collided with another train. Part of the train then fell down an embankment. *The Times* of 6 March said that an inquiry was expected. The Clapham inquiry was still going on and had entered its third week. The headline of *The Times*'s report said, 'Channon tries to restore confidence'. Paul Channon was the secretary of state for transport.

Conservative MPs were concerned about overcrowded trains and believed that an inquiry was needed to restore public confidence. Michael Portillo had visited the scene of the crash at Purley and was anxious to restore public confidence. It seems that railway safety had become a political issue, with comments from all sides of the House. Opposition parties put the blame for a decline in railway safety down to government cuts.

The Clapham Junction accident of 1988, when thirty-five people died. (Mirrorpix)

Calls for investigations into the accident were repeated in *The Guardian*. They described the accident as a new crash horror only three months after Clapham and that it was most important that it was investigated very quickly.

Overcrowding was obviously a big problem on trains. When a train's brakes failed and it hit buffers at Cannon Street Station on 8 January 1991 it had only been travelling at 5 miles an hour. There were still two deaths and more than 200 injured. The train was carrying about 1,000 passengers when it should only have had 800 seated and eighty standing, so many were standing at the time of the collision.

The train, the 7.38 am from Sevenoaks, was also thirty years old. It took emergency services more than three hours to release 200 passengers who were trapped. The driver blamed the train's brakes. The previous day, British Rail had been committed for trial at the Central Criminal Court for failing to provide an effective signalling system at Clapham in 1988.

When two people died at Greenock on 25 June 1994 there was little blame that could be placed on British Rail. According to *The Times*'s report of 27 June the death of the driver of the Wemyss Bay to Glasgow train and a passenger were classed as murder. The train had been derailed by concrete blocks deliberately placed on the line. The police made house-to-house investigations on the nearby Peart Road Estate.

219

Severe damage to a modern engine but there is no information as to the site of the crash. It was claimed that the train involved was travelling too fast.

After the Clapham Junction accident in 1988, the number of those killed in rail accidents declined. When five people were killed on 15 October 1994 at Cowden it was the highest number killed in an accident for more than five years.

The 8.00 am train from Uckfield to Oxted and the 8.04 from Oxted to Uckfield collided head-on. The accident happened on the only remaining diesel-operated single line on Network South East. The trains should have passed on a dual track further south. Both trains were late but the northbound train should have waited at Ashurst for the other to pass.

The Guardian explained that the area had been a double line until 1991, when it was converted to a single line to save money on maintenance costs. The move had been opposed by locals, who claimed a collision was inevitable.

There was a strange finding in the Department of Transport report. Major Holden, who wrote it, found that the driver of one of the trains was responsible but that there was insufficient evidence of unlawful killing. There was some suspicion that the guard may have been driving the train.

Another accident occurred in London when, on 19 September 1997, six people died in an accident at Southall. A passenger train from Swansea to

Another modern engine with severe damage but again, with no clue as to the place it happened.

✗ SAME AGAIN

Another mystery engine with severe damage.

London passed a danger signal and collided with a goods train crossing its path. According to *The Times* of the following day, the driver of the passenger train was arrested for manslaughter. He was breathalyzed at Southall police station.

The Times's report mentioned that the driver of the train involved in the Purley accident in 1989 had been sent to prison for manslaughter. The safety of railway travel was still being used as a political football, with a spokesman for the RMT rail union saying that the sell-off of British Rail in 1995 may have contributed to the accident.

There were further deaths on the London railways when, on 5 October 1999, thirty-one people died at Ladbroke Grove after a head-on collision. The train caught fire and many of the passengers were unable to get out without breaking windows.

The Guardian of 7 October had a headline saying: 'The signal was red but the train sped on'. The accident had been confirmed as being caused by the driver of the 8.06 commuter train passing a signal at red. Although the points were against it, the weight of the train forced the points open and allowed it to run into the 6.03 am express from Cheltenham.

There was a comment in the report of how inexperienced the driver who passed the red signal was, and it looked as though blame was being put on him. He died in the crash. It seems that there had been a number of complaints about the signal, which was very hard to see. It had been involved in eight incidents in the past six years but Railtrack had taken no action.

The Ministry of Transport report said that signals may be missed when the driver was looking at cab displays or controls. There was much made in the report of the tests taken to find the suitability of a man to be a train driver. It also mentioned that the driver had only been qualified for thirteen days.

There was only one train involved in the next fatal accident. Part of a train was derailed at Hatfield on 17 October 2000 and led to four deaths. Although vandalism was at first suspected, the fact that the front of the train passed safely seemed to disprove this. There were then fears of a bomb on the line, but it was thought to have been a broken rail that caused the latter part of the train to come off the lines.

The train was the King's Cross to Leeds express and was travelling at high speed when the accident happened. Three coaches turned over and four others came off the line. The final coach seemed to have been the one that suffered the worst damage.

The Guardian reported on 18 October that safety on the railways was under scrutiny again. It is interesting to note that reports into rail accidents now seemed to have the names of four reporters on them.

After a decrease in the number of serious accidents, they were now happening at the rate of at least one a year. On 28 February 2001 ten people died at Selby after a car ran onto the track and was hit by a passenger and a goods train. *The Guardian* declared: 'Tragedy returns to the tracks'. Inadequate crash barriers on the motorway at Selby were thought to be to blame. The driver of the car had managed to get out before the train hit it. An express from Newcastle to London hit the car and then went head-on into a coal train.

There was a serious accident at Potters Bar on 10 May 2002, when seven people died. Again, there was only one train involved when a carriage on the King's Cross to King's Lynn train became derailed and rolled onto the station platform at 12.55 pm. Those waiting on the platform had to run out of the way. The injured had all been in the last carriage of the train.

One of the fatalities was the husband of author Nina Bawden, Austen Kark, who was the director of the BBC World Service. Bawden was also seriously hurt in the accident. Part of the wreckage hit the parapet of a bridge, which then collapsed. The seventh victim was not a passenger but a pedestrian, Agnes Quinlivan, hit by falling masonry from the bridge.

The cause was thought to be a fault with a set of points. *The Times*'s report of the 11 May said that this would be a disaster for Railtrack, which was now in administration because of the neglect exposed by the Hatfield accident that had occurred only a few miles from the scene of this one.

The report by the Health and Safety Executive in May 2003 found that the points were poorly maintained. Some bolts holding the stretcher bars were

The Selby accident of 2001. Ten people died when a train hit a car on the line. (Mirrorpix)

The Potters Bar accident of 2002. Seven died and seventy-six were injured. (Mirrorpix)

loose or missing. The points had been examined twice a few days before the accident by workers from Jarvis, the private railway maintenance company. Earlier that evening a railway worker had reported serious vibrations on the line at the same point where the accident occurred. It seems that the information was passed on but workers from Jarvis were sent to the wrong location and did not find the problem.

There were claims that the condition of the points was due to sabotage by Jarvis but no proof was found. The HSE later found that a number of points in the area were also in a poor state of maintenance.

Nina Bawden, writing in *The Times* in May 2003, said, 'In our privatized railway system no one reported potential safety defects properly.'

According to *The Guardian*, the travelling public were once again presented with scenes of appalling devastation. The rail network was in fresh crisis. It seems that *little had changed in more than 160 years.*

The effects of the Potters Bar crash went on for many years after the event. It looked as though Jarvis would be charged in court but this took so long that after the company went into administration in 2010 charges against them were dropped. It was not until 2011 that Network Rail was fined £3 million over the accident.

CHAPTER 15

Conclusion

The development of rail travel in Great Britain led to some unexpected issues that went beyond the sole subject of transport. There was obviously going to be a certain amount of danger related to a form of transport using previously unimagined levels of power and moving at speeds that mankind had never experienced before.

This new form of transport also led to some unexpected consequences. The origins of what has become known as a compensation culture can be found in the mid-nineteenth century, when it became possible to claim for damages against railway companies. This led to a specialization in a type of medical expertise, with doctors writing books and concentrating on the type of injuries suffered in railway accidents. This became a lucrative source of earnings for these expert witnesses, the railway injury specialists, and for their opponents, who were often doctors employed by the rail companies themselves and were therefore in conflict with colleagues from their own profession.

There was also a great deal of work for solicitors in these new court cases. In early inquiries into railway accidents it was common for the rail companies but not the victims of the accidents to have legal representation. The introduction of compensation for these victims was perhaps the main reason that they eventually began to be represented as well.

The danger associated with rail travel has always been greatly exaggerated when one considers the number of accidents in relation to the number of rail journeys actually undertaken. This has been said often but the fear of accidents has still been promoted by the coverage of these catastrophes in the press. Early press stories often dwelt on the grisly results of rail accidents.

There seems to have been two main categories of causes of accidents. One is failure of the mechanical operations of the train or of what the trains ran on, such as rails, bridges or the signals that were supposed to warn of danger. The second is those caused by human error on the part of signalmen, drivers or others employed on the railways.

Accidents as a result of the first category were much more common in the early days of rail travel. This was often due to the failure of the materials that were used to make the hardware of rail equipment - often down to a lack of knowledge and experience in producing materials that were fit for the use they were put to.

This obviously improved with the use of steel over cast iron and developments in engineering. It is rare for bridges to collapse today as they did in the early days although there have been some more recent accidents due to the failure of rails, especially before rails were continuously welded.

Along with the accidents came something that must have caused terror in anyone trapped in wreckage: fire. This was often caused by the gas used to light carriages but the change to electric did not eradicate the danger. The introduction of diesel engines added a new danger of fire.

Human error is something that is more difficult to overcome. There have been factors that have magnified this, such as fog and even the blackout during the war. Improvements in signalling and safety systems have gone some way towards nullifying human error. The use of a dead man's handle can even overcome the sudden incapacity of a driver.

As the records show, however, there have still been accidents in recent times due to human error, especially when drivers have passed danger signals either by mistake or taking a chance that has resulted in serious consequences.

Although the number of serious accidents has declined those that have occurred more recently have often been more serious. It is impossible to say that further accidents will not occur. There is also the added danger of terrorist attack on railway systems such as the London Underground, although this is not an exclusively modern problem as there were Fenian attacks as far back as the nineteenth century.

The Irish Republican Brotherhood had begun in America and had its first meeting in London in 1861. Its members were known as Fenians. Violence by the society's members began in London shortly after the first meeting in the city. In 1867 there was an attack on London's Clerkenwell Prison in an attempt to release a Fenian member being held there. The resulting explosion demolished six nearby houses and killed six people.

A number of bombs were exploded in Britain during the Fenian bombing campaign of 1881 to 1885. The year 1883 was to see the first Fenian bomb attack on the London Underground when a train travelling between Charing Cross and Westminster was targeted. There were a number of injuries. Further Fenian bomb attacks on the London Underground were carried out in 1884 and 1885.

CONCLUSION

Despite the dangers the introduction of rail travel was one of the most important aspects of turning our country into a unified community. It made travel and communication between remote parts possible. It also did much to advance the Industrial Revolution by allowing important goods such as coal to be moved to places it was needed quickly and cheaply.

Despite the rarity of serious accidents on the railways today they still arouse a great deal of attention when they do occur. They may not attract huge crowds of spectators as they did in the past but there can be few who are not interested in the story or photographs of accidents.

Perhaps it's the fascination with the risk of being involved. Many people use the railways on a regular basis. You expect to get on a train and get off safely again at your destination. When an accident happens there is a lingering anxiety about how close you could have been to being involved in it yourself.

Bibliography

Books

Conner, J.E., *The Wreck of the Cromer Express*, Connor & Butler Ltd, Colchester, 2003.

Erichsen, J.E., *On Railway and Other Injuries of the Nervous System*, Henry Lea, Philadelphia, 1867.

Extracts From Rule Book, British Railways Board, 1972.

Facts About British Railways in Wartime, British Railways Press Office, 1943.

Faith, N., *Derail: Why Trains Crash*, Channel Four Books, 2000.

Fletcher, J.O., *Railways in their Medical Aspect*, J.E. Cornish, London, 1867.

Freeman, M. & Aldcroft, D., *The Atlas of British Railway History*, Croom Helm, 1985.

Hall, S., *Danger Signals*, Ian Allen Ltd., London, 1987.

Hamilton, A.M., *Railway and Other Accidents with Relation to Injury and Disease of the Nervous System*, William Wood & Co., New York, 1905.

Hamilton, J.A.B., *Britain's Greatest Rail Disaster*, George Allen & Unwin Ltd., London, 1969.

Hamilton, J.A.B., *Disaster Down the Line*, Javelin Books, Poole, 1987.

Hamilton, J.A.B., *Railway Accidents of the Twentieth Century*, George Allen & Unwin Ltd., London, 1967.

Hamilton, J.A.B., *Trains to Nowhere*, George Allen & Unwin Ltd., London, 1981.

Kingdom, A.R., *The Railway Accident at Norton Fitzwarren*, Ark Publications, Newton Abbot, 2005.

Lewis, Peter, *Beautiful Railway Bridge of the Silver Tay*, Tempus, Stroud, 2004.

Page, H.W., *Railway Injuries*, William & Wood, New York, 1892.

Rolt, L.T.C., *Red for Danger*, Sutton, Stroud, 2007.

Searle, M., *Down the Line to Southend*, Batton Press Ltd., Kent, 1984.

Reports (in chronological order)

Selby Board of Trade Report, Lieutenant Colonel Sir Frederick Smith, 1840.

Sonning Board of Trade Report, Lieutenant Colonel Sir Frederick Smith, 1841.

Rockcliffe Board of Trade Report, Captain J.L.A. Simmons RE, 1849.

BIBLIOGRAPHY

Burnley Board of Trade Report, Captain George Wynne RE, 1852.
Atherstone Board of Trade Report, Colonel W. Yolland, 1860.
Shipton-on-Cherwell-Board of Trade Report, Captain H.W. Tyler, 1865.
Newark Board of Trade Report, Colonel W. Yolland, 1870.
Inverythan Board of Trade Report, Major F.A. Marindin, 1882.
Armagh Board of Trade Report, Major General C.S. Hutchinson RE, 1889.
Norton Fitzwarren Board of Trade Report, Colonel F.H. Rich, 1890.
Chelford Board of Trade Report, Major F.A. Marindin, 1894.
Cudworth Board of Trade Report, Major General J.W. Pringle, 1905.
Salisbury Board of Trade Report, Major General J.W. Pringle, 1906.
Ditton Junction Board of Trade Report, Lieutenant Colonel H.A. Yorke, 1912.
Quintinshill Board of Trade Report, Lieutenant Colonel E. Druitt, 1915.
Abermule Ministry of Transport Report, Major J.W. Pringle, 1921.
Naworth Ministry of Transport Report, Lieutenant Colonel A.H.L. Mount, 1926.
Leighton Buzzard Ministry of Transport Report, Lieutenant Colonel A.H.L. Mount, 1931.
Battersea Ministry of Transport Report, Lieutenant Colonel A.H.L. Mount, 1937.
Norton Fitzwarren Ministry of Transport Report, Lieutenant Colonel A.H.L. Mount, 1940.
Ilford Ministry of Transport Report, Lieutenant Colonel G.R.S. Wilson, 1944.
Harrow and Wealdstone, Ministry of Transport Report, Lieutenant Colonel G.R.S. Wilson, 1953.
Dagenham Ministry of Transport Report, Brigadier C.A. Langley, 1958.
Knowle & Dorridge Ministry of Transport Report, Colonel D. McMullem, 1963.
Hither Green Ministry of Transport Report, Colonel D. McMullen, 1967.
Ealing Department of Enviroment Report, Colonel I.K.A. McNaughton, 1973.
Taunton Department of Transport Report, Major A.B.G. King, 1978.
Polmont Department of Transport Report, Major A.B.G. King, 1984.
River Towy Department of Transport Report, A. Cooksey, 1987.
Cowden Health and Safety Executive Report, Major C.B. Holden, 1994.
Ladbroke Grove Health and Safety Executive Report, 1999.

Journals & Newspapers
Aberdeen Weekly Journal: 21 October 1878; 9 August 1881; 17 July 1884; 10 June 1892; 29 March 1900; 18 June 1900.
BBC History Magazine: September 2012; December 2012; January 2013.

Berrow's Worcester Journal: 27 May 1847.

Birmingham Daily Post (The): 25 August 1858; 5 September 1860; 5 August 1863; 8 June 1865; 1 July 1867; 22 June 1870; 28 November 1870; 13 December 1871; 4 August 1873; 12 September 1874; 9 August 1876; 29 December 1879; 12 August 1880; 4 June 1884; 10 June 1892; 13 August 1892; 14 August 1893.

Blackburn Standard (The): 21 December 1836; 25 August 1858.

Bradford Observer (The): 28 January 1874.

Bristol Mercury (The): 16 September 1854; 25 November 1882; 2 January 1885; 3 November 1892; 3 September 1898.

Bury and Norwich Post (The): 3 September 1861; 11 November 1890.

Cheshire Observer: 10 June 1865; 13 August 1892.

Current Archaeology: October 2012.

Daily Gazette (The): 27 August 1875.

Daily News (The): 12 February 1849; 8 September 1851; 4 August 1852; 16 July 1852; 14 September 1855; 30 June 1857; 17 November 1860; 26 August 1861; 17 December 1862; 21 August 1868; 11 October 1869; 3 October 1872; 4 August 1873; 28 January 1874; 25 December 1874; 22 January 1876; 25 December 1876; 17 September 1887; 16 January 1890.

Derby Mercury: 26 May 1847; 3 December 1873.

Dundee Courier & Argus: 21 August 1868; 27 December 1870; 30 December 1879.

Essex County Standard: 11 September 1874.

Evening Gazette (The): 7 December 1870.

Examiner (The): 19 September 1830; 23 August 1840.

Freeman's Journal (The, Dublin): 21 August 1868.

Glasgow Herald (The): 12 February 1849.

Guardian (The): 17 July 1961; 29 December 1962; 3 March 1967; 15 March 1967; 1 August 1967; 6 November 1967; 7 January 1968; 8 May 1969; 12 June 1972; 20 December 1973; 1 March 1975; 8 June 1975; 7 July 1978; 20 December 1978; 2 March 1979; 17 April 1979; 23 October 1979; 12 December 1981; 1 August 1984; 13 October 1984; 5 December 1984; 27 July 1986; 20 October 1987; 22 October 1987; 13 December 1988; 5 March 1989; 9 January 1991; 22 July 1991; 27 June 1994; 16 October 1994; 20 September 1997; 6 October 1999; 18 October 2000; 1 March 2001; 11 May 2002.

Huddersfield Daily Chronicle: 28 November 1882.

Illustrated Police News: 2 November 1872.

Jackson's Oxford Journal: 1 January 1842.

Lancaster Gazette: 3 August 1850; 22 June 1876.

Leeds Mercury (The): 11 October 1869; 30 October 1872.

Liverpool Mercury (The): 11 June 1847; 2 May 1851; 25 December 1874.

Lloyd's Weekly Newspaper: 20 October 1878.

Manchester Guardian (The): 28 July 1903; 24 December 1904; 28 July 1905; 2 September 1905; 30 January 1910; 24 January 1911; 18 September 1912; 3 September 1913; 19 June 1914; 2 January 1915; 5 January 1915; 18 December 1915; 20 January 1918; 21 February 1922; 1 March 1922; 4 November 1924; 31 August 1926; 20 November 1926; 15 February 1927; 25 August 1927; 28 June 1928; 10 July 1928; 9 June 1929; 21 November 1929; 23 March 1931; 26 March 1933; 7 September 1934; 29 September 1934; 16 January 1936; 3 April 1937; 11 December 1937; 28 December 1940; 5 November 1941; 31 December 1941; 31 December 1942; 17 January 1944; 18 January 1944; 3 June 1944; 5 February 1945; 19 April 1948; 22 March 1951; 22 September 1951; 9 October 1952; 9 April 1953; 6 August 1953; 24 January 1955; 21 November 1955; 3 December 1955; 5 December 1957; 30 January 1958. Post 1958 – *see Guardian (The)*; *The Manchester Guardian* became *The Guardian* in 1958.

Morning Chronicle (The): 14 December 1836; 14 November 1840; 28 December 1841; 18 June 1847; 15 May 1848; 9 September 1851; 25 August 1858; 26 August 1861.

Morning Post (The): 14 December 1836; 10 August 1840; 2 May 1851; 8 September 1851; 15 July 1852; 29 June 1857; 26 August 1861; 4 August 1863; 8 June 1864; 14 June 1897.

Northern Echo (The): 22 June 1870.

Newcastle Courant: 2 January 1879.

North-Eastern Daily Gazette: 15 May 1883; 13 June 1889; 11 November 1890.

Observer (The): 25 December 1910; 27 July 1913; 23 May 1915; 15 August 1915; 14 October 1928; 16 June 1939.

Penny Illustrated Paper (The): 28 January 1905; 7 July 1906; 23 September 1906; 29 September 1906; 5 June 1907; 19 October 1907.

Reynold's Weekly Newspaper: 23 December 1897.

Sheffield and Rotherham Independent: 11 October 1869.

Standard (The): 16 November 1840; 25 December 1841; 13 September 1855.

Times (The): 8 October 1829; 18 September 1830; 26 November 1832; 14 December 1836; 24 June 1840; 10 August 1840; 12 August 1840; 27 October 1840; 13 November 1840; 14 November 1840; 10 September 1841; 11 September 1841; 20 September 1841; 25 December 1841; 1 January 1842; 18 June 1845; 14 October 1845; 27 December 1845; 21 January 1846; 23 September 1846; 24 September 1846; 27 January 1847; 2 February 1847; 12

May 1848; 13 May 1848; 11 September 1848; 20 September 1848; 13 February 1849; 2 August 1850; 3 August 1850; 23 September 1850; 24 September 1850; 2 May 1851; 7 June 1851; 9 June 1851; 8 September 1851; 25 November 1851; 26 November 1851; 8 March 1852; 9 March 1852; 15 March 1852; 15 July 1852; 5 August 1852; 6 August 1852; 12 August 1852; 26 August 1852; 29 November 1852; 6 December 1852; 25 December 1852; 5 January 1853; 25 February 1853; 28 February 1853; 7 March 1853; 6 October 1853; 7 October 1853; 6 December 1853; 14 September 1855; 18 September 1857; 29 June 1857; 30 June 1857; 25 August 1858; 26 August 1858; 5 September 1860; 6 September 1860; 17 November 1860; 19 November 1860; 26 August 1861; 27 August 1861; 3 September 1861; 4 September 1861; 15 October 1862; 5 August 1863; 8 June 1864; 17 December 1864; 9 June 1865; 10 June 1865; 13 June 1865; 29 January 1867; 1 July 1867; 21 August 1868; 11 October 1869; 22 June 1870; 23 June 1870; 29 November 1870; 5 December 1870; 14 December 1870; 28 December 1870; 29 December 1870; 30 October 1872; 4 August 1873; 3 December 1873; 28 January 1874; 12 September 1874; 25 December 1874; 26 December 1874; 30 August 1875; 22 January 1876; 24 June 1876; 9 August 1876; 25 December 1876; 26 December 1876; 21 October 1878; 29 December 1879; 12 August 1880; 10 August 1881; 28 November 1882; 16 May 1883; 4 June 1884; 2 January 1885; 17 September 1887; 1 April 1889; 13 June 1889; 14 June 1889; 5 March 1890; 12 November 1890; 10 June 1892; 4 November 1892; 14 August 1893; 25 December 1894; 11 November 1895; 12 November 1895; 7 April 1896; 14 June 1897; 4 January 1898; 6 September 1898; 18 October 1898; 29 March 1900; 18 June 1900; 28 July 1903; 24 December 1904; 20 January 1905; 28 July 1905; 2 September 1905; 2 July 1906; 21 September 1906; 29 December 1906; 16 October 1907; 22 April 1909; 26 December 1910; 24 January 1911; 18 September 1912; 3 September 1913; 19 June 1914; 2 January 1915; 24 May 1915; 16 August 1915; 18 December 1915; 4 January 1917; 27 September 1917; 21 January 1918; 28 January 1921; 4 November 1924; 31 August 1926; 20 November 1926; 15 February 1927; 25 August 1927; 29 June 1928; 10 July 1928; 15 October 1928; 9 January 1929; 21 November 1929; 23 March 1931; 26 May 1933; 7 September 1934; 29 September 1934; 17 June 1935; 16 January 1936; 3 April 1937; 11 December 1937; 5 November 1940; 3 July 1941; 5 November 1941; 31 January 1942; 4 February 1944; 3 June 1944; 5 February 1945; 2 January 1946; 25 October 1947; 28 October 1947; 18 April 1948; 17 March 1951; 22 September 1951; 9 October 1952; 9 April 1953; 6 May 1953; 16 August 1953; 24 January 1955; 20 November 1955; 3 December 1955; 5 December 1957;

31 January 1958; 22 January 1960; 17 July 1961; 27 December 1962; 16 August 1963; 29 May 1964; 1 March 1967; 6 March 1967; 1 August 1967; 6 November 1967; 7 January 1968; 5 January 1969; 8 May 1969; 3 July 1971; 2 June 1972; 31 August 1973; 20 December 1973; 1 March 1975; 7 June 1975; 7 July 1978; 20 December 1978; 17 April 1979; 23 October 1979; 12 December 1981; 31 July 1984; 5 December 1984; 27 July 1986; 20 October 1987; 13 December 1988; 5 march 1989; 22 July 1991; 16 October 1994; 20 September 1997; 6 October 1999; 18 October 2000; 1 March 2001; 11 May 2002; 8 July 2003; 16 February 2004; 7 November 2004.
Western Mail: 29 December 1879.
York Herald: 30 December 1879.

Places to Visit

For a list of UK rail museums, visit the website:
http://en.wikipedia.org/wiki/List_of_railway_museums_in_the_United_Kingdom

For a list of steam railways and heritage centres, visit the website:
http://en.wikipedia.org/wiki/List_of_British_heritage_and_private_railways

Index

Discover Your History

Ancestors • Heritage • Memories

Each issue of *Discover Your History* presents special features and regular articles on a huge variety of topics about our social history and heritage – such as our ancestors, childhood memories, military history, British culinary traditions, transport history, our rural and industrial past, health, houses, fashions, pastimes and leisure ... and much more.

Historic pictures show how we and our ancestors have lived and the changing shape of our towns, villages and landscape in Britain and beyond.

Special tips and links help you discover more about researching family and local history. Spotlights on fascinating museums, history blogs and history societies also offer plenty of scope to become more involved.

Keep up to date with news and events that celebrate our history, and reviews of the latest books and media releases.

Discover Your History presents aspects of the past partly through the eyes and voices of those who were there.

FREE
BOOK
WHEN YOU
SUBSCRIBE TO
Discover Your
History

UK only

Discover Your History is in all good newsagents and also available on subscription for six or twelve issues. For more details on how to take out a subscription and how to choose your free book, call 01778 392013 or visit **www.discoveryourhistory.net**